See Me Now
From Invisible to Invincible

JANET RAVENSCRAFT

Copyright © 2015 Janet Ravenscraft

All rights reserved.

ISBN: 069246462X
ISBN-13: 978-0692464625

TABLE OF CONTENTS

	TABLE OF CONTENTS	Pg # iii
	ACKNOWLEDGEMENTS	Pg # v
Chapter 1	WHEN I FIRST BECAME INVISIBLE	Pg # 1
Chapter 2	BECAME A HABIT	Pg # 19
Chapter 3	HOW I FOUND MY WOO	Pg # 37
Chapter 4	QUIET OBSERVER ON BULLYING	Pg # 53
Chapter 5	INQUISITIVE – FINDING THE ANSWERS	Pg # 67
Chapter 6	GLASS HALF FULL - POSITIVITY	Pg # 85
Chapter 7	STRENGTHS VERSUS WEAKNESSES	Pg # 93
Chapter 8	SEE ME NOW	Pg # 101
Chapter 9	INFORMATION FOR YOU	Pg # 119
Chapter 10	BOOK RECOMMENDATIONS	Pg # 123
	DEDICATION	Pg # 125
	ABOUT THE AUTHOR	Pg # 127

Janet Ravenscraft

ACKNOWLEDGMENTS

I would like to recognize those who have helped me along the way starting with Patricia Noel Drain, who without her assistance as my business coach, I would have never even known I had a book to write. Luckily, she's a patient woman, who encouraged, empowered and pushed me along.

Next, Renee Settle, stepped in and told me in the beginning you have a powerful story to tell, but it feels like you stop when it gets less than rosy. She was right, the blue skies and sunshine part of me didn't want to visit the dark side and just moved on when the skies turned grey. With her support and developmental editing, I was able to forge through the tough times and finish this book. On top of that, she formatted and took on the publishing side, when I was totally in over my head and couldn't have done it without her. I am forever grateful for her encouragement, attention to detail, and the friendship that has happened along the way.

A special shout out to Jessica Abbott, who I met last year at a networking event, where we both weren't in the mood to network, so we sat there, drank wine, connected and now we are forever friends. She has been instrumental in guiding me along, trying to teach me the basics, answering my millions of questions, designing my website and providing vital input, as I was trying to navigate the technical waters.

I can't leave out my family. They've always been my backbone and source of love and solace when I needed it and I can't tell you how lucky I am to have them all in my life. First and foremost, my husband, John, has never wavered in his love, encouragement and support on all my crazy ideas or latest project I have wanted to have him build for the last 43 years. This last year, he has been there believing all along, I was going to write this book and that he'll be carrying my books, as we travel the world and I tell my story. What a guy!

Janet Ravenscraft

My kids Joel and Jenna, are my heart and soul. I tell them there is nothing like the love of a child or the love for a child and how I cherish every moment I get to spend with them. I am blessed to be there Mom.

Also, I would like to acknowledge my parents. I hope you feel like you know them, somewhat, from reading my book. I always knew I was loved even when I was my most invisible. I loved being my daddy's girl, who was my hero and biggest supporter my whole life. When he passed away in 2009, it was a devastating blow to my heart, as I just figured he would live forever. I miss him more than I could have ever imagined. Thankfully, Ma is still here with us all and shows us daily what unconditional love looks like. I am one lucky woman to have all these wonderful people and more in my life.

Finally, to all of you out there I have had the privilege of knowing and to those of you I have yet to meet, I am grateful every day for the life God has given me and can't wait to see you again, share a hug, or get my first hug; enjoy.

With gratitude and joy, find your magic, wonder, and endless possibilities!

Janet Ravenscraft

CHAPTER 1
WHEN I FIRST BECAME INVISIBLE

"I don't need a cloak to become invisible."
~J.K. Rowling

Here's my story . . . when I was young, we moved a lot. I mean, really a lot. I went to 8 different grade schools, including two kindergartens. They weren't even across town or in the same state--we moved from the East Coast to the West Coast and back by the time I was five.

Some of my earliest memories are riding in the back seat of our car. They were always big, old cars, with doors that were too heavy to open on my own and lots of huge windows to look out. In fact, I usually couldn't reach the door handles and if I could the door was too heavy to open or close it. I remember, we had a red and white Oldsmobile, with this enormous back seat, that if I wanted to even look out the windows I had to stand up or at least be on my knees.

We roamed the back seat to see out or leaned over the front seat to see where we were going. Sometimes it was just too much whizzing by and I'd just have to lie down and close my eyes for a while, as it felt like too much and I was overwhelmed. My heart would be pumping and I could hear it in my ears, as I lay on the back seat. I always felt safer with my eyes closed and I'd just listen to my breathing and my parents talking in the front seat.

This is when I remember first thinking I was invisible and no one could see me, if my eyes were closed. If I was with my parents, I'd feel a calm wash over me and I felt loved and happy. If I was alone, in my bed and would get scared of the dark or something that was happening, I also thought I was invisible if my eyes were closed. I'd squeeze them so tightly shut and pull my favorite pink, blanket up close to my face covering it. Sometimes holding my breath until the feeling either passed or I'd finally get the courage to jump out of bed. I'd either run to my parents room or go find them in the house, just so I could feel that love, security and happiness again. It's so interesting to me how those feelings can all come back to me this many years later.

Of course when we were in the car, I'd generally fall asleep with the motion and humming noises, waking up later either at home or where we were going that day. To this day, closing my eyes relaxes me and helps me get balanced and centered and I still usually drift off to sleep if I'm in the car.

For long trips when we were young, the back seat would be built up with blankets and pillows all the way across, so my younger brothers and I could see out, play and sleep. It felt like we would drive for days always going someplace on what my dad would call "Our Adventures." I'm sure this is where I get my need to travel and see new places.

Sometimes we'd wake up in a gas station in the middle of the night or early morning. We'd get out in our pajamas to stretch and get a snack and use the bathrooms, whether we needed to or not. The next morning, we'd change our clothes in the car or in a gas station or restaurant bathrooms and my Mom would always do my hair and wash us up for the day.

On our first coast-to-coast trip, my middle brother and I were both under 5 and my youngest brother wasn't even born yet, so my parents had their hands full. Plus, that was before seat belts or car seats and there were no tablets with movies and gadgets to keep us entertained, we had to find things to do ourselves and when you're little that isn't always so easy.

During the day we'd stop sometimes to have lunch picnics just to get us out of the car. I remember one time in particular when we stopped for lunch. It was summer and we were all hot and cranky. Our car didn't have any air conditioning, so we had been riding with the front windows partially down blowing hot air all around us.

Rest stop areas back then didn't usually have tables and restrooms; they were just pullouts alongside the road or highway. My dad didn't stop until he found a shady spot that day. It felt so good to get out of the car and stand up and stretch, as my little body was sore from being in the car all morning. There was a small patch of grass that felt cool to my hot feet. The sun was peeking through the trees and there was a slight breeze, I just closed my eyes and stood there for a couple of minutes, relishing the quiet and the soft, cool breeze.

Then my mom called, as she was spreading out the blanket for us to sit on and started making sandwiches. She'd packed a loaf of bread, peanut butter and jelly and made them while we waited. Peanut butter and jelly sandwiches were always my favorite and I was hungry, so it tasted even better. My dad cut up some apples and oranges that tasted sweet and cool. They only brought things along that didn't need to be kept cold, as this was before coolers and ice that makes traveling these days so much easier. Our juice was warm in the jar we shared, but still tasted good there in the shade that day.

Soon my mom was telling us to finish up that we needed to get going. We didn't stay too long as we always had to get someplace. We usually only stopped to get gas and eat, then back in the car and on the road again, where we'd play with our toys, colored, slept and watch the world go by.

On that same trip west, on our last day going over Donner's Pass, we ran into a freak summer snowstorm that shut the highway down for several hours. I remember the snow swirling around outside my window and not being able to see very far, only the cars in front and back of us. We were going really slow for a while then stopped altogether.

It was summer and so hot when we started out that day that we were all dressed in summer shorts and tee shirts. My dad had turned the heater on earlier when it started to snow, so the inside was warm and comfortable, until he had to turn the engine off when we stopped. Since it was summer, we didn't pack any really warm clothes for the trip.

I remember my mom rummaging through the suitcase trying to find some warmer clothes for all of us. My brother and I ended up in our pajamas over our summer clothes, with socks, sandals and sweatshirts. Luckily, since the back seat was built up with blankets, my mom crawled in the back with us and we snuggled under the blankets to keep warm, while my dad got out to see if he could find out why we were stopped.

It was fun for a while, as my mom tried to keep us entertained; however, as you can imagine after a couple of hours with two toddlers stuck in the back seat of a car, with little food and no way to get out and run around for a bit, was not a great afternoon for any of us.

We spent several hours stopped in the middle of the highway that day with everyone else. The snow and fog were so heavy and just kept falling, that it made everything muffled and seemed so far away. Especially when the windows fogged up it felt like we were the only people in the whole world. It was scary and I remember crawling under my pink blanket where I felt safe and warm.

I remember people were in and out of their cars, walking back and forth, just checking on each other. My dad would start the car engine every hour or so to warm the interior a bit, then turn it off to preserve the gasoline. I remember standing outside our car door with a blanket wrapped around us, taking bathroom breaks and my dad going to find some clean white snow to melt for water in our jars.

Once the storm stopped, it still took the rest of the day to get all the cars moving again. Of course, no one had any snow shovels with them, so everybody improvised with what were in their cars at that time. Buckets, plastic bowls, hats, boxes, suitcases anything that would help them dig the cars out of the snow banks.

I just remember the snow being up to my waist when I got out of the car and I couldn't walk in it, just crawled across the top. My brother and I were put up on the snow bank, while my parents dug our car out. It was fun and noisy with lots of people talking loudly to each other, while everyone was helping, so we could all get off the mountain that day finally. I remember some cars that had run out of gas and were pushed off to the side. It was quite the adventure that day and something I have remember my whole life, the snowstorm on Donner's Pass.

Until I grew, up I thought everyone traveled that way. We never stayed in a hotel and while one parent drove the other one slept. Once I remember waking up and we were parked alongside the road. It was quiet as I was coming awake and I could hear birds singing that wasn't a normal sound in the morning. The sun woke me up first, as it was streaming through my window, warm on my face. I sat up and rubbed my eyes, but I wasn't sure where I was, I just knew it wasn't my bed.

As I peeked over the front seat, I was a little scared because my parents weren't moving, until I heard my dad snore and I realized they were sleeping. I touched my dad on his shoulder and he sat right up, smiled at me, stretched and said "Good morning Sissy Sue, did you sleep well?" then he woke my mom up. I loved my dad's nickname for me, as it always made me feel special and loved. Even when I felt my most invisible, I knew he was always there for me.

There on the side of the road, we changed out of our pajamas, washed up and got ready for another day on the road. This was our way of life and by the second trip back across country we were veterans and knew what to expect.

My first real memories start when I was about 3 years old. My middle brother and I are 21 months apart, so I became a big sister before I was three and I took that responsibility very seriously. When my mom would go out of the room, she would say to me, "Watch your brother, so he doesn't get into anything."

He was my quiet, laid back, easy-going brother, who never rushed, forever taking things apart trying to figure out how they worked and a daydreamer. I remember dragging him along because he was so slow, helping him finish putting away his toys, finding all the pieces of something he took apart or getting dressed.

He often wandered off some place and I would be sent to look for him or told to keep an eye on him, while my mom did some chore. Sometimes I would get scared when I couldn't find him right away. I would worry what if he was hurt, because I didn't keep a close eye on him.

One time when we were at the next-door neighbor's house playing, he crawled up and sat down in one of the old type lawn chairs, with the arms that lifted up to move the back up and down. He somehow got one of his small fingertips pinched off. He never cried, just showed me and stuck his hand under his arm. I remembering grabbing his other hand and dragging him down the alley to our house. I was crying and screaming all the way so by the time we reached our yard my mom and the landlady were rushing towards us.

They were sure that I was hurt in some way, because I was the hysterical one. My mom was down on her knees shaking me to try and get me to stop crying and kept asking me where I was hurt. My little brother just stood there with his hand under armpit. I'm crying and pointing to him, when my mom finally looked at him and he pulled his bloody little hand out.

Then everyone went into action. When I told them what happened someone went and found his tiny little fingertip, wrapped it in a towel and stuck it on ice. My mom had cleaned his hand off and wrapped it in ice and a towel; too, before we headed to the hospital. Luckily, the doctor was able to sew his fingertip back on.

Even though no one ever blamed me and it's has always been referred to the "accident", as his big sister, I just knew it was my fault and I should have watched him closer. This one incident was the beginning of reinforcing my need to take care of others and has become a lifelong trait. As I have been writing this book, so many things have become clearer for me and the process has helped me to understand why I have created some of these needs, strengths and habits of mine.

###

The first time my dad was in the Navy that I remember,

we were stationed in Michigan. We lived in a small, two-bedroom house, just outside the military base gate. There were these huge, metal gates on enormous hinges that were always open when we went on base. I would look up at them and wonder how hard it would be to close them. I liked the soldiers at the gates when they stood at attentions and would salute some of the cars. I'd press my face against the window to watch them. Sometimes they would wink at me as I was looking out the window riding by. They wore clothes like my dad did and I trusted them.

My brother and I shared a room with our beds under the window that we could look out and see who was coming to our house. It was always bright in our room at night from the lights on base. I liked it that way, because I could see everything in our room and there were no dark places.

I especially remember this room when both my brother and I had the chicken pox at the same time and spent several days in our beds, being cranky and splotchy from the calamine lotion our mom and dabbed on us and wanting to scratch so bad, that mom ended up putting socks on our hands.

My dad sometimes walked to work, if my Mom needed the car, as we only had one and they didn't always start. It seemed like we were always getting another old car. They were all so big, especially when I stood next to them and looked up. I was too small to see in the windows or usually couldn't reach the handles.

Everything seemed big to me then, I was always trying to reach something; doorknobs to open, shelves to get my books or toys, drawers to find clothes to wear or put away, refrigerators to get something to eat or drink, couches and chairs, just trying to get up on them was a chore. My memories as a young child are probably a lot like yours, as we were learning new things every day and there was so much we didn't know.

This is where I experienced my first tornado warning and being truly afraid. The sirens would usually go off in the middle of the night and wake us out of a sound sleep. I'm sure there were warnings during the day, however I only remember the night ones. We would be pulled out of bed, dressed; all the while the sirens were blaring. I would cover my ears and sometimes cried not knowing what to expect. I remember I had small red suitcase that we always brought with us. It was packed with clothes and things we may need, if we couldn't go back home right away.

One night, as we went out in the dark night I remember, I looked up at my Mom, with her scarf on her head and her coat not buttoned and she looked worried to me. She had my infant brother in one arm and was holding tight onto my hand in the other. I was dragging the red suitcase behind me and she was telling me to, "Hurry." We headed for the field behind our house, while it rained and the grass was wet on my feet.

I didn't like the dark or the lightening or the rain or my mom being scared. I could feel it in her hand as she held mine tight and pulled me away from my warm bed and the safe haven of my room. I could hear it in her voice as she coaxed me along, while both my brother and I cried.

We would be rushing and sometimes the wind was blowing so hard that we struggled to get to the trenches. When I would look around everyone was in a frantic hurry, with babies crying and people trying to talk over the storm. All rushing through the night and their shadows would stand out each time the lightening lit up the sky, in flashes, like an old-time movies reel.

We were crouched down in the trench, huddled together with my mom. The noise of the wind crashing through the night, with leaves and branches swirling around, made me cover my head and hide under my pink blanket. I closed my eyes and snuggled under my mom's arm, escaping into my invisible world where it was calm and comfortable.

As my dad would often be required to be on base to secure the planes and equipment, I don't remember very many times that he was with us during these raids. Luckily, while we lived there we never actually had a tornado hit the base area, however just the fear of the unknown, at such a young age was the beginning of feeling that deep down fear inside, that just made me want to disappear and be invisible.

Being scared of the dark continued for me, when my dad was transferred to San Diego and we lived in old Quonset hut buildings on another base. These were temporary facilities for families waiting for permanent housing to become available. We were in a two-bedroom unit that had a round roof and set up in a long row with a unit facing us in the other row.

The interior walls didn't go all the way to the ceiling, so there was always light over the top with shadows and movement. I never liked that place we lived in, as my memories are of a place dark and full of shadowy areas. I can remember lying in my bed and my brother already asleep. I'd be watching the lights above the wall from the other room and I would conjure up images and figures that would scare me and make me cover my head with my blanket until I feel asleep.

My dad found out the ship he was stationed on was scheduled to go out to sea soon, while we were still living in those Quonset Huts on the base, waiting for permanent housing. Our friends we were stationed in Michigan with were now in San Diego, too, and he was on the same ship with my dad. They were my Aunt Bonnie and Uncle Jim and it was decided by both families, that we would live together with our moms and my two cousins Debbie and Scott, while our dads were gone to sea.

My dad met him when he first joined the Navy and then we were all stationed together in Michigan, where both of them had been born and raised. Our moms became best friends and my brother, Steve, and cousin, Scott, were both born, while we were stationed in Michigan.

Our families became friends and extended family for a lifetime. At that time, Debbie was less than a year older then I was and Scott was close to the same age as my brother Steve. We shared rooms, clothes, toys and life experiences. I had just started kindergarten, so my cousin and I went to school together each day.

With all the changes in those last few months and not really understanding why my dad was gone. I kept asking, "Where's daddy? When's he coming home?" I missed him terribly and didn't know why he wasn't there. I started school and it was foreign and confusing. I always felt loved and secure with him and he was gone. I didn't know anyone and since there were no pre-schools programs in those days, a classroom setting was another unknown that frightened me.

I remember my cousin being so much more confident then I was and would take my hand when I would hesitate or be afraid to do something. She would encourage and stand by me, always being very kind and considerate of my feelings. Her mom liked to sew and made us these matching dresses and took a picture of us. The picture brings back fond memories of that time together and I cherish our lifelong friendship.

There were four of us kids, six and under, so our moms

tag teamed us and we did everything together. My Mom and Aunt equally loved and scolded us. We were brought up to respect our elders and behave any adult that told us to do something. We didn't argue or talk back that was disrespectful and unacceptable.

When my dad came back from sea, we moved into a house down the street from my cousins for a few months, before my dad decided to get out of the Navy and go back to college. My Mom was pregnant with my youngest brother that winter and was having a difficult time. The doctors told her that a long road trip would be too hard on her and the baby, so we took our first airplane ride back to the East coast. We had to leave a few months before my dad was released, as my mom couldn't fly any later in her pregnancy.

We packed up all our toys and clothes again and were told we were going to see my Nana and live there for a while. This was in the middle of kindergarten for me, so I would finish the second half on the East coast and became the beginning of going to new schools each year for me. Plus, we were leaving my cousin and her family to go live with a Nana I could hardly remember. I had just got comfortable and we were moving again.

We could only take a few of our toys and clothes with us, and were told my dad would bring the rest with him when he drove back by himself. I was so happy when my dad came home from sea, it felt so good when he hugged me and I had missed him terribly. Now I was told he wouldn't be flying back with us, that he had to stay and work. I was so sad that we were leaving him and I didn't understand why he couldn't come with us on something called a plane ride.

I remember standing in line on the tarmac getting ready to board the plane and being scared. I had my little red suitcase that had my favorite pink blanket, a few toys and clothes for my Mom, brother and I. It was heavy and I was afraid to let go and lose it. The plane was so big and there were so many tall people, all talking at the same time. I was still upset that my dad wasn't coming with us and it was a tearful goodbye. Things were changing again and I didn't understand what was happening.

My Mom was several months pregnant, not feeling her best and traveling with two small children. It was a very long day, with several plane changes and we were tired and everyone was cranky. The last flight was at night and awful!! There was a bad storm with rain, thunder and lightning that lit up the sky and plane and it made so much noise.

The three of us were sitting together in the same row, with me by the window. It was so dark outside and I could see the lightning when it flashed and it would make me jump. It had been a very long day and I was really tired. I wasn't sure I liked planes very much, as they were all bumpy, noisy and I couldn't move around, as I had to wear a seatbelt.

The storm was causing so much turbulence that we all were suffering from motion sickness. I remember trying to hold my little airsick bag over my mouth, while being bounced around. We were a pitiful trio, all of us sick, including my mom who could hardly help herself no less my brother and me. I just wanted to get off that plane.

Luckily for us, there were two sailors sitting in front of us that turned around during the worst of the flight. I remember looking up and they were smiling and had such kind eyes. They both helped my brother and I hold our bags and they talked to us, trying to distract us and make us laugh. They were our saviors that night and we always talk about how grateful we were that they were on our flight.

As my dad was getting his college education, we lived with

family and friends off and on during those early years, which included summers in my relative's basement, while my dad worked as a roofer for my uncle. Then during the school year, we lived in college campus housing, where we shared rooms and moved each year. I do remember becoming possessive of my few belongings that I was able to take to the different places we stayed. I didn't want to let them out of my sight or to forget them when we moved on.

As the oldest of three and the only girl, my parents' hands were full. My dad was a full-time student who worked part-time jobs and studied in between. I remember him being gone when we woke up in the morning, then coming and going during the day and being tired a lot. He tried to be home for dinner and before we went to bed, so he could spend a few minutes with us.

He wasn't the grumpy type and must have studied between classes and after we went to bed, because we never had to be quiet for him, only when my baby brother was sleeping. My Mom was always busy with the three of us, and my youngest brother still in a crib. She sometimes worked for the college part-time, when we were in school and would take my baby brother with her. She also babysat for other students, especially after school was out until their parents got home, so we always had extra kids around.

Early on, I learned to be the good girl, did what I was told and stayed out of the way. I knew I was loved and cared for. However, I was a very shy, non-demanding, and still scared of the dark kind of child. I remember keeping quiet and believing I was invisible even when I had my eyes open. I didn't always feel like I fit in or belonged at my new schools.

Those of us whose parents were in college tended to stick together, but those friendships didn't last long either, as our families were always moving, as our parents changed schools, dropped out or finally graduated. It was hard to always be the new girl, especially when many of the other kids had been together before and already knew each other.

By the time I was in 2nd grade, this was my fourth school and I was perfecting the art of being invisible. There was always a lot going on at school--so what if the new girl was quiet and shy? I didn't ask many questions or get called on, so I could be as invisible as I wanted. It was easier than trying to get attention, making new friends or getting someone to listen to me. I felt lonely and safer, staying in the background not being noticed. There were enough kids in my classes who demanded attention, so those of us who didn't, could stay invisible.

In addition to being the new girl who was shy and quiet, I wasn't very coordinated or athletic either. I dreaded whenever teams were selected for the playground or classroom, as it was agonizing to often be the last or next to last kid picked. I knew I didn't ever want to be a captain or a person in charge. It was too much responsibility and I was no leader of others.

I didn't sparkle with confidence and energy or felt I was able to meet other's expectation. I didn't feel confident enough to volunteer or push to the front of the line yelling out, "Pick me, pick me!" What if they laughed at me or told me, "You can't do it because you're not good enough."

When there was lots of chaos, especially with two younger brothers who demanded more attention, I could be overlooked at home, too. Not in a cruel way, it was just the average day-to-day happenings in a busy household. I remember that it was important for me to make sure our toys were put away, because if they weren't we'd all be scolded and I as the oldest felt responsible.

My parents only had to tell me a few times that I was the oldest and needed to set a good example for my younger brothers. I was so tenderhearted, that the least little look of disappointment or reminder devastated me. One of those times when I knew we were going to get into trouble, because our toys hadn't been picked up, I burst into tears and started to cry as soon as my dad walked in. He didn't even have to say anything to me and I was blubbering and picking up our toys crying the whole time.

I knew early on I wanted to do whatever I was told, so I could avoid the look. I always wanted to be told I was a good girl and never wanted to make my parents mad or disappointed in me. I always wanted to please them. This wasn't ever anything I talked to them about or even recognized in myself when I was that age.

I can remember, when I was around 8 years old and having nightmares that would paralyze me. I shared a room with my brother and we had two twin beds on either side of the window. My bed was on the same side as the door. I had been scared of the dark for several years and we always slept with a night light in our room. Sometimes I'd wake up in the middle of the night, seeing shadows on the walls and door.

One night the light was coming in from the window and through the trees shifting and changing with the wind. My imagination created scary figures on the door I needed to go past to get to my parents room. I sat up and tried to call out and when I opened my mouth and yelled nothing came out. I was shaking so hard and I was so scared, but I just couldn't get out my bed.

I finally couldn't stand it any longer and jumped out of bed, staying as close to the bottom of my bed, until I could scurry out the door and ran to my parent's room. I cried and refused to go back to my own bed that night. It felt so cozy and safe in that double bed with the three of us. This happened several times, while we lived in this house, to the point I remember my dad going to sleep in my bed some of the times.

When my dad finished Junior College, he transferred to the University. By the time he graduated with his degree, we had moved six more times, including summers at my relatives'. Once he had his business degree, of course we moved again to another state. As my dad was trying to start a new career competing with graduates who were ten years younger, I was starting over in another new school at ten years old, still feeling awkward and out of place.

When I was young, I didn't know why I felt so distant and was more comfortable being invisible. I couldn't see what it was or explain it to others, as they were overwhelming feelings that were all bottled up inside me. We can see and hear the differences in the ways others talk, dress, or walk; however, why someone is shy, lonely, scared or introverted is different in each person. I often felt like I was the only one who felt lonely and scared. I never even considered that many of my classmates might have had the same feelings of loneliness and being afraid.

My Advice to You:

Since your personality, habits, values and outlook on life are developed at an early age, take the time to find those things that you like to do and make you feel good. As parents, help your children find their values and strengths. When you have a shy, introverted child, see if you can find something they excel at and help build their confidence in that area. Once they have confidence in one thing, it may help them decide to try something new.

As for moving, this is a stressful time for the whole family, including kids and animals. Be aware and talk about everyone's fears and concerns. Give your kids time to adjust and say goodbye to their friends. See the resource page for articles and websites for further information.

Janet Ravenscraft

CHAPTER 2
BECAME A HABIT

"The chains of habit are too weak to be felt until they are too strong to be broken."
~Samuel Jackson

The summer I turned 13, we moved again from the East Coast back to the West Coast. Another adventurous road trip, this time crammed in the back seat of our red station wagon, with the back part packed to the ceiling. We weren't little kids any more that would nap during the day; and with no air conditioning, while traveling in the middle of summer again we were hot and cranky.

Just before the trip, I remember when my parents sat the three of us down to tell us that we were moving again and that my dad was going back into the Navy. I didn't really know what that meant exactly, but I did like it when he had put on his white sailor uniform and hat that day, because he looked all clean and shiny and happy. My favorite part was when he slid his hat back on his head, smiled and gave me a big hug.

Even though my dad gave the best hugs and I would do anything for him, I didn't want to move again and he knew it. I had just finished the 6th grade and I had made a few friends, who I rode bikes with and we'd meet at a tree between our houses. We'd crawl up into the tree, hang out and swap notes. I remember one spring day just after school, getting on my bike and riding to meet my friend at our tree. It was actually a dead tree with the top branches cut off. This left a hollowed out area up where the branches started to spread out. It wasn't too tall, so we could easily climb up in it.

As I rode up on my bike that afternoon, I was so excited because no one was there and I had the whole tree to myself. This was a popular tree with the neighborhood kids and it was first come - first dibs. I jumped off my bike and scrambled up in the tree, so happy with myself and I couldn't wait to share it with my friend. I leaned back against the branch and closed my eyes feeling the warmth of the sun on my face and the rough textured of the bark at my back. In that moment, I was happy and content and everything was perfect in my little world.

I really liked our house and neighborhood and school wasn't too bad. I had my first male teacher and didn't dread going to school each day. I even had my own bedroom for the first time. Our house was a big, old, white colonial style place, with 3 stories, counting the basement. The main floor had a huge country kitchen with a dining room and large living room. It was a house that we could spread out in and everyone had space. Plus, we had this cool sunroom that we used as a playroom. We finally had a place for all of our toys and books and games and didn't have to pick them all up each night, we could just close the door.

My room was on the third floor and I could look out my window and see over all the houses and some of the trees. I remember sitting by my window and being able to watch the sunset and dream about traveling to faraway places. My bed was an antique set that had been in my dad's family and belonged to my grandparents. It was an intricately carved Cherry oak headboard and baseboard that matched the carvings on the dresser drawers and mirror frame. Plus, it had this full piece of pink marble for the dresser top. I loved this bedroom set and it was all mine. It was the first time I felt like I fit in somewhat. Now we were moving again and I was going to have to start all over someplace else. I knew what that meant and I was sad, scared, angry and unhappy.

On the trip that summer, in the back seat that was still built up to be flat across with our blankets and pillows; we fought for space, complained about the heat, tried to sleep, were bored and kept asking, "Are we there yet?" My youngest brother, John Willard, was in the middle and was ADD and Bi-Polar before either of those diseases were even a diagnosis. He was 7 and this was his first coast-to-coast trip and by the 2nd day he was done with the back seat and traveling. Since my middle brother, Steve and I were older we got to sit by the windows and that's all he wanted to do was be by a window. He kept crawling back and forth from window to window like a caged animal. He fidgeted, whined and cried the whole afternoon.

Driving through the desert, during the day, the air was so hot it felt like my nose was on fire and nothing but sand and more sand. With the scorching, sun beating through my window, I was so hot that I just knew I was going to melt into one big puddle there in the back seat. Okay, remember I was 13 and couldn't help myself being a drama queen and I really didn't want to move again.

The three of us bickered, argued and guarded our spaces in that back seat - that day. We of course didn't even want to touch each other, which was tough in an area that was getting tinier with each mile we traveled. I even sat in the middle for a while just to get my little brother to stop whining and of course that only lasted for a short period of time.

It felt like the longest day ever and when we finally stopped for dinner that evening. No one spoke to each other for the whole time. My brothers both had their heads down shoveling food in their mouths. My parents were both tired and while my dad looked at the map my mom had both hands wrapped around her coffee mug staring off in space. It was quiet and blissful for the first time all day! Then we changed back into our pajamas for the night and crawled back into the back seat of our car with the promise of being there tomorrow.

My parents didn't have it any easier as they drove straight through that summer, switching off driving, listening to us complain and fight with each other and trying to get some sleep before they had to drive again. They were as glad as us kids to finally get there and when we all piled out of the car at our friend's house, it was with relief and extreme happiness to have that trip over.

So by the time we got to California, we had a month to find a house, get unpacked and settled in, all before school started. I was numb by this point and just did what I was told. I was still sad and scared, not knowing what was going to happen. Old habits; of biting my nails, not sleeping and being anxious came back with a vengeance. Our new house was very small, but at least, I still had my own room and my brothers shared one again.

A lot happened in that month, we had traveled over 3,000 miles, settled into another new house, and getting prepared to start at another new school, so getting acclimated and finding our way around was on the bottom of the list. I dreaded school starting and not knowing anyone. I knew this feeling well and it filled me with fear and anxiety.

My brothers seemed to roll with it and made friends in

our new neighborhood. I hadn't met anyone starting junior high and felt so alone and isolated again. I hid my feelings and reverted to being quiet and as invisible as possible again. Wrapping myself in that familiar cloak of invisibility gave me some type of comfort and helped my world to stop spinning and slow down for a few minutes. My fear was raw and felt painful as my heart ached.

Everything changed for me that summer. I was used to living in an area with all four seasons, in a large city, that was very green, with lots of trees and hills. Because of all the hills and dense vegetation, you couldn't see long distances and everything felt close together, especially with all the big, old buildings. We even wore more clothes and never went anywhere without a jacket or sweater.

Now I felt like we had one season and it was summer; there were wide-open spaces, big blue sky, no buildings over two stories and lots of funny looking palm trees. Everything looked light and breezy, like it would fly away on the next puff of wind, just like the life I knew. I had absolutely no reference or concept of what to expect or how to act.

It was finally my first day of junior high school. Do you remember your first day of junior high? How'd this happen? In sixth grade, I'd finally reached the top of the heap. You know when you feel comfortable in a place and the younger kids looked up to you and needed your help. I had a great 6th grade teacher, had made a couple of friends and I knew pretty much how to maneuver around the different cliques and groups to just be there and not be picked on or noticed.

I remember not always wanting to be invisible that year, even though I was still not very athletic, shy, somewhat introverted and just an average student. My bullying was subtle. I wasn't picked on or teased like my little brother; it was more being ignored or not seen, which would increase that feeling of being invisible for me.

So my first day of junior high was painful. On top of everything else, I had grown during that summer to my full height of 5'8". With everything else going on I hadn't even realized I'd grown taller, as my clothes still seem to fit me, just shorter. For a girl who made a habit of running under the radar and working really hard at being unnoticed, I couldn't hide, and stuck out like the proverbial sore thumb.

That first morning I dragged myself to the bus stop, even though the sun was shining bright and I could hear birds singing and there was this nice ocean breeze, I felt so out of place and uncomfortable. As I looked around, I was taller than anyone else standing there, so I slouched to be as small as possible and stood on the outside of the group. I overheard one girl say, "She's so tall." and another girl whisper, "I wonder if she's a new girl, I've never seen her before?"

I remember trying to casually look around so no one would notice, to see if anyone else was standing alone or was I the only one, yet I knew I would never approach them or start up a conversation for fear of being ignored. No one approached me that morning, so it just reinforced my habit of thinking that something was wrong with me. I felt isolated and alone standing in that group of kids, wanting to be anywhere else right then.

I missed my old school and the few friends I had. I thought to myself, " At least I would know someone if we hadn't moved." It was the one thing I could control, when I was invisible and I felt like they just couldn't see me then I didn't feel as bad and it was better than being ignored all by myself. It reminded me why it was so much easier to be invisible than trying to get someone's attention and try and fit in where I didn't know the rules or expectations.

By the time I got to school, I was a sweaty mess, especially since I was dressed for the East, not West Coast weather. I was so out of place. My outfit consisted of a longed sleeved blouse, skirt and sweater, socks and sturdy shoes. Most of the girls were in summer outfits looking cool and comfortable, with cute little summer shoes, so while I was limp from the heat and uncomfortable in my heavy clothing they were having fun and getting reacquainted with their friends.

Then I had to learn how to get around an outdoor school set-up. I was used to big, old brick buildings that were two and three stories tall. This was all outside and spread out. We did gym outside and we had to wear these funny, white, bloomer type suits. What?? How could a tall girl stay invisible in a gym suit and have time to change and shower between classes? This didn't happen in elementary school. The first week was a nightmare full of stress and scary moments. I remember being late, disheveled and scatterbrained for my class after P.E. for most of that week. It didn't feel like anything was working right for me.

Plus, now I had six periods of classes and six new teachers, not just one to figure out and stay out of their line of vision. My classrooms were all over the campus, some hard to find and everything seemed so foreign. The classroom buildings were in long rows with sidewalks in front and lockers on one end, then the next row of classrooms were attached by another sidewalk. It was so confusing and the worst part was I now had a locker with a combination that I had to remember several times each day, unless I wanted to try and carry all my books all day long. It was all so overwhelming.

On my third day of school, I still hadn't met anyone from my neighborhood who rode my bus, so I went as late as possible, so I wouldn't have to stand by myself. I'd walk slowly, until I heard the bus, then rush and be the last person on the bus and sit by myself.

When I got to school that day, I headed straight for my locker and kept repeating my combination in my head. The day before I had trouble getting it open a couple of times, so I was nervous. The lock was the kind built into the front of the locker, not a padlock, however I doubt that would have mattered, as I couldn't get it open. I remember leaning my head against the locker, sweating and ready to cry. I knew the tardy bell was going to ring any moment and I would be late.

There was lots of noise, with kids talking and slamming lockers, but all I could hear was my heart beating. I thought to myself,

"Please open locker, please, please, please open."

"Why won't you open . . . I hate you locker!"

"Oh no, I'm going to be late again."

I must have looked like I needed help, as one of the teachers tapped me on my shoulder. As I turned to look down at her, she was a tiny little thing who seeing the look of absolute terror on my face, figured out quickly I couldn't get my locker opened. Lucky for me, she had a master key and opened it right up. Her parting words to me were, "Honey, just write the combo down in your notebook. It'll be easier by next week." And that's exactly what I did.

I had nightmares for years about forgetting my combination and being late for class. Plus, I now had two lockers, one for my books and one for my gym class. I soon found out that Physical Education was my worse class and I dreaded going each day. Not only did I have to undress and change into that hideous gym suit, I also had to participate in some type of sport activity each day. Playing Kick the Can and Hide and Go Seek, with my cousins, never prepared me for organized sports.

Some people are born with athletic ability and I unfortunately wasn't one of them. I had a hard enough time before I had grown the two inches over the summer. My height only made me stand out as a bigger target and higher expectation from others. Now when I ran, I was all gangly legs that went every which way than the direction I wanted them to go. I stumbled and tripped my way through class every day. I remember basketball being the hardest and my teammates learned quickly not to pass me the ball, as I couldn't dribble and run at the same time or make a basket.

Every day is a challenge for the uncoordinated and any Physical Education class is no exception, as the teachers have to require everyone to participate and no one wants you on their team, so it's double the pressure. I remember the feeling of failure and humiliation as I waited, while captains picked teams, knowing I would be picked last or next to last. The worst part were the groans I would hear from the better players, who didn't want me on their team.

It's not like I didn't know I couldn't keep up with them, however to have them ridicule and be angry with me was difficult for a girl who already had low self-esteem. It was better to stay invisible; since that was the only tool I knew to protect myself from the mean girls.

The next year of junior high was more of the same. Maneuvering the campus became easier and I went out of my way to help the new 7th graders find their way around. They were more scared than I was and never ignored me. They were just grateful someone saw them and helped them find their way.

The best thing that happened to me in the 8th grade was when I broke my wrist one day in my Physical Education class. We were playing basketball, of course, out on the tarmac and I tripped running down the court. As I was falling

I stuck out my left hand and heard it snap. Once I had that cast on, I was able to dress down the rest of the year and not have to try and keep up or listen to my teammates complain about me. It took the pressure off me to try and compete each day and made the rest of 8th grade bearable.

###

The next year, I started a four-year high school and went back to the bottom of the heap again. It was just a bigger environment and being invisible was a habit by then that I used often. I circled and flitted from group to group, even joining a few clubs that were non-threatening, and continued to stay out of the way. To get out of ever having to take another Physical Education class, I joined the school marching squad. They weren't discriminating on who could be a member and in high school I was no longer one of the tallest kids in class, so I wasn't as self-conscious of my height.

The first week was pretty easy and it was so much better than the Physical Education class I would have had to take, so I just went along with the group. The older girls were all friendly and helped us on and off the field. No one yelled or made fun of anyone else, we practiced, learned routines and bonded. This was by no means the most popular group of girls, but we were all there for our own reasons and it became one of my favorite classes during the day, because it felt safe and comfortable, giving me some place to look forward to going.

On the night of the first home game, as we were marching in and everyone was so excited, it hadn't all really sunk in for me; that I had joined a group that would be performing on the football field . . . at half-time. . .in front of the whole school. All of a sudden I was terrified, there were so many people in the bleachers, standing by the fences and walking round and making so much noise. What was I thinking??

I felt like I was going to throw up!

"What if I tripped?"

"Fell down?"

"Forgot my routine or just plain messed up?"

"What if . . . ?"

In that moment I pulled out my habit of closing my eyes and blocking everything else out. I remember standing with my eyes closed, until the band started and we were supposed to march in, then I focused only on the girl in front of me. I followed her until we sat down.

During our half-time routine I did the same thing and followed the girl in front of me hoping she knew what she was doing as this was so much more than I had anticipated. I never looked up.

I turned when she did . . . I walked when she did.

I never heard the band playing . . . and followed her when we marched off the field.

After I survived that first night and even though I had experienced all that fear and anxiety, I knew I had figured out a way to be part of this group. Besides, it was still better than going back to a regular Physical Education classes.

My Mom grew up in the 30's and had a tough childhood. She even moved out on her own when she was 13 years old. Getting herself a job at the local diner and living above it until she graduated from high school. School, her friends and that tiny community nurtured and supported her, so she always talked about how much fun high school was for her. She was so excited for me to experience it, because of her fond memories.

I remember one evening, as she was getting ready to go bowling with my dad, I was standing in the bathroom talking to her. I was a head taller than she was, so standing behind her, I was looking over the top of her head in the mirror, as she was putting her hair up in a French twist. She wanted to know when the first school dance was and her eyes sparkled, as she started talking about some of the dances she'd been to and how much better high school was than junior high. She was smiling at me in the mirror as she was reminiscing about dancing with her friends, then going to the diner after the dance and how much fun they all had laughing and talking together. She was so enthusiastic about the friends I was going to make and the fun I was going to have, that I remember thinking, "Maybe it will be different in high school."

Then I went to my first dance.

A few of the girls were going from the marching group and invited me along. Their energy was high, so it made me want to have high expectations that night, too. It was held in the high school gym, so it was a big room with part of the bleachers pulled out. It was a cool evening and I wore a dress I hadn't worn to school yet. I remember laughing and enjoying myself dancing with the other young girls for a while.

As the older kids showed up, several as couples, the atmosphere in the room changed and the younger kids backed up to give them room, then as the lights went lower, the band started to play a slow song. One by one the other girls I was standing with went to dance or visit with other friends and all of a sudden I looked around.

I was standing alone.

As I was backing away from the dance floor, people were going by me laughing and having fun. Panic set in. "Was I invisible??" I wasn't trying to be at that moment, but it felt like I was, as kids pushed by me like I wasn't there. I didn't see anyone I knew, so I went and sat up in the bleachers by myself. When the band took a break later and the lights came up some, I went back down and stood with some of the other girls again, but it wasn't the same. I was now anxious and nervous and soon the lights went back down. No one asked me to dance, so there I was again standing by myself in the sea of music, and people. I was feeling lonely and invisible.

Once I was back up in the bleachers, I couldn't make myself come back down until the dance was over. All the fear and anxiety came flooding back as I was watching everyone else have fun, dancing, laughing and teasing each other and here I was sitting in the bleachers by myself thinking to myself;

"Where was the fun?"

"Why didn't I feel like I belonged?"

"Why didn't anyone ask me to dance?"

"What was wrong with me??"

As the last song was being played I left the gym and went out to look for my dad who was picking me up. I was quiet and still kind of perplexed when I got in the car, so when my dad asked me "How was the dance?" I told him "Fine." then I turned and looked out the window until we got home. I just didn't know what went wrong and kept going over the night in my head to try and figure it out. Plus, I knew my mom would be waiting up wanting to know all about the fun I had, so I was trying to figure out what to tell her that didn't sound pathetic.

Always the girl who wanted to please everyone, I didn't want to disappoint my mom by telling her how awful the dance really was and how lonely and out of place I felt. I told myself it must have been my fault, because other people were having fun, so I must have done something wrong. What was I going to say??

As I knew she would be, my mom was waiting at the door and I seriously couldn't tell her the truth. I remember telling her it was fine and that I was tired and wanted to go to bed. She followed me into my room still excited about my first high school dance and not understanding my reluctance to share with her. She finally hugged me and went to bed. In my bed that night, I went back over it all again in my head trying to figure out what I did wrong. Questioning every word I said, what I wore, how I wore my hair and compared myself to the other girls there that night until I finally feel asleep.

###

Since dating is such a large part of high school, I was like most young girls looking forward to that first crush, boyfriend, date, kiss, etc. Well that wasn't my life and those like me will understand the loneliness and isolation you feel. I never had a boyfriend and only had a couple of dates. I had crushes on boys who never returned the feelings. I yearned to be part of a couple and not a third wheel. I blamed myself and knew I must be doing something wrong.

Depression set in during this time. It took control of my emotions and outlook on life throughout high school. I didn't really know what was affecting my moods and causing the sadness and emptiness I felt, as it wasn't a common ailment anyone talked about then. It was hard to be upbeat and positive when I didn't feel like I belonged. I was lonely and sometimes felt like I was on the outside of some window watching my life happen. Not being part of it.

During this time my Mom was sick and in lots of pain. She became distant and unapproachable, as she was dealing with her health problems, surgeries and recovering from her own ailments. I became more sullen, slept a lot, got by in school and even had a bout of mononucleosis in my junior year that kept me out of school for a few months. By now it didn't matter to me, if I went to school or not.

It was actually easier to just be home in my room listening to music or sleeping. My brother Steve was a freshman in high school, so he brought my schoolwork home for me weekly. Very few people came to see me while I was out of school, which just made me feel more invisible and isolated than ever. They had lives and boyfriends and school events to be involved in and I felt like I was easily forgotten.

When I went back to school, it was still more of the same. The depression, loneliness and low self-esteem all settled in and it felt like this was my destiny to feel this way. I remember thinking, "If this is all it was ever going to be, then why bother making an effort. Is this really all there is?" The depression was so debilitating and all-consuming at times, it took away my will to care, even though I still tried to keep busy. I remember mostly just going through the motions, always looking for things to do, because I knew I only felt worse if I did nothing.

So, in school, even though I very rarely volunteered for anything and if a teacher was asking for help, I'd put my head down and pretend like I didn't hear or was busy reading, writing or looking for something, I'd still find things to do or finish other people's task. Being idle was something I fought against, as I figured out keeping busy helped to defuse the depression for a while. If I saw something that needed to be done, I just did it.

I joined the Booster Club, because they let me paint signs and finish art projects for the school. We made big signs for the fences and walls at football games and school events. I can't tell you how many after schools hours I spent finishing signs all by myself that other people started. They'd show up, work for a while or mostly spend more time laughing and talking, then leave early.

I remember one afternoon after school I was out on the sidewalk in front of the art room, finishing up signs by myself. I was tired and frustrated and had been talking to myself for the last half hour about how nobody cared what I did, so why did I bother.

That afternoon the head football coach stopped by, as he was heading home after practice, and looked around. He wasn't one of my teachers, however we had met the week before when I had made some copies for him and finished collating one of his a booklet, while helping out in the office.

He asked, "Where is everyone else?" I was surprised to see him and quipped back, "I was wondering the same thing where were all the people who indicated they would help?" He told me, "I appreciate what you're doing here and that you care enough to stay and do it by yourself."

From that day forward, I respected and admired him, because he encouraged and listened to me. Since I had an open class period, I volunteered to be his aide and we got along famously. He was a big man, who didn't smile often, but when he did it lit up his face. It always made me feel good when I made him laugh or at least smile, as I knew he wasn't easily amused and didn't do it often. He was a tough master and worked his football players hard, yet he was kind and gentle with me.

As his aide, his coaching staff knew they could depend on me to assist their programs. I paid attention, listened and anticipated what needed to be done next, often before they could ask. Because I was resourceful and self-reliant, I could usually figure out how to complete tasks on my own. Because I was always fighting the depression looking for things to keep me busy and asking what I could do next, they gave me projects or left me notes and assignments.

The head coach and I were an odd alliance, yet he saw my confidence and self-worth increase as he encouraged me and gave me projects that I could experiment with and excel in. He had a football banquet every year and my senior year he let me plan and organize it. He trusted my abilities to complete any task; therefore, I believed I could do anything he gave me. I had the best time working on that event. I was creative and made football centerpieces and signs, covering the tables and decorating the cafeteria like it had never been decorated before, making it the best banquet that year.

The highlight that night for me was receiving an appreciation plaque from the football coaches. They recognized my efforts to get the school ready for home games, and what I did for the football program. I wasn't a cheerleader, didn't date any football players, or held any council position; I just helped them because they appreciated me as a person. The reason I helped them is that they recognized me and I wasn't invisible to them.

My Advice to You:

Learning to be self-reliant, resourceful and figure things out on your own are great self-confidence builders. Create habits that are positive and find things that you are good at and like to do. Focus on those traits that are fun and give you joy. Surround yourself with people who enjoy life and are supportive.

If you or someone you know experiences long periods of depression, feelings of despair or hopelessness, you may need to seek professional help. In my experience, depression isn't something that just goes away on its own, most people need help. Adolescent depression is the most common factor that leads to teen suicides. Feelings of hopelessness and anxiety, along with feeling like they are trapped in a life they can't handle, are very real contributors to teen suicides.

Teenage and high school angst is alive and well and something we all have experienced or will. It's not easy even for the most positive and confident teen to maneuver high school and the teen years, no less those with low self-esteem and self-worth. Everyone has his or her own high school horror stories and we all do what we have to get by some days. We are shaped by our experiences, good and bad, bringing many of those coping skills learned with us into adulthood.

What seemed like the end of the world at 16, when we look back after 5, 10, 20 years later we can laugh at some, however there may still be hurt and confusion left from others.

We all have our own "stuff" that we have nurtured and carried with us our whole lives. It's not necessarily good or bad it's just ours. This book is my attempt to look at my life and find those things that helped me to be the positive, productive, loving person I am today and expand on those skills. It has also helped me identify those traits that aren't my favorites, pin-point where they came from and decide how I can either improve on them or let them go.

Everyone should stop at some point in their life and look at their "stuff". For me it's been profound, answered lifelong questions, empowering and eye-opening being the best thing I have ever done for myself.

CHAPTER 3
HOW I FOUND MY WOO

"The Art of WOO: Winning Others Over is a powerful tool that can make a significant difference in your work, life and in the lives of those around you. Use it wisely and use it well."
~Daniel Decker

This was my foundation -- how I developed and became this person who had low self-esteem, bad posture, limited social skills, and usually feeling like I didn't fit in anywhere. WOO was so far out of my realm of thinking and functioning daily, that it was such a surprise when I found out what it was and how it worked for me.

I was still suffering from bouts of depression and I remember when I couldn't sleep at night I would climb out of my bedroom window and walk to the beach. I lived about 10 blocks from the beach and as I would get closer to the ocean I would get in rhythm with the waves. Sometimes I would just sit, listen and breathe. It was calming and relaxing for my body and brain. Other times I would spend hours walking and thinking just trying to tire myself out, so I would sleep when I got home.

I had no idea what I wanted to do after high school. I didn't explore many options and, truthfully, I didn't even know what I wanted to do next. I hadn't even had a job yet. College didn't interest me, as I had no idea what I wanted to study and I was done with the whole trying to fit in socially. In the 70's, girls weren't actually encouraged to go to college unless they wanted to be nurses, teachers or needed specific training. I was raised to get married, have children and support my husband.

I got my first part-time job that summer as a restaurant hostess working weekends. It was a busy place and I realized quickly if I smiled, was nice and friendly to the customers and my co-workers I would have a better day versus the days when I was quiet, distracted or depressed.

I remember one Sunday morning getting in early and deciding to be in a good mood that day, no matter what. The day before had been boring and people were cranky and it was a long stressful shift. As I walked in that morning, I pasted a big smile on my face and greeted everyone I saw with that smile and tried to say something nice to each of them. I had been listening to one of the waitresses that week as she always tried to notice something nice about her customers and enjoyed telling them. She was always happy, enjoyed her job and made great tips, so I thought I'd try it.

It took some effort on my part, as I wasn't used to starting up conversations or paying too much attention to other people. I generally avoided eye contact and kept quiet, so I wouldn't be noticed and stayed in the background being as invisible as possible. This day, I was determined to make it a good one and see how many people I could compliment and make smile back. I started with the babies and little kids, as they were the easiest to get to smile and most of the parents would smile if I spoke to their little ones.

Once I got started I had fun and noticed as I included my co-workers and customers that they were having fun, too. I remember my managers telling me he liked the new, happy me, and he hoped to see that same happy girl next weekend. I went home that day with a smile on my face and knew it was because of my choice to be happy and have fun at work that day. It took away the depression for a few days and made me look forward to going back to work. The next weekend, I went back in with that same positive attitude and started a new habit of observing and looking for nice things to say about people.

It was difficult and a little scary for me at first, putting myself out there and being open for others to respond back to me, however I soon realized that if I said something positive and nice most people would respond accordingly. This was a new concept for me that made me feel good and gave me a way to interact with others. The best part was, I found the more positive I was each day that the bouts of depression were getting less. I liked the way it made me feel all bubbly and lighthearted. I found I liked to laugh and when others laughed with me it was fun and I would get excited to do it again.

My parents, in their wisdom and experience, knew I still needed some type of training in a field or trade that interested me. I had no specific area that I wanted to know more about, so they researched and found a one-year program that would give me an interior design certificate; however, it was really more for the finishing school, also known as Charm School.

According to Google, these schools were originally designed for young women, as a completion of their education to focus on their social skills and cultural norms for entry into society. These schools provided marriageable women with training in social graces and to become accomplished in the art of running a home.

These schools continued to evolve, adapt and upgrade their systems and criteria focusing on Social and Business Etiquette, Image Development, Posture and Presence, Presentation Skills, Health and Self-Esteem for the current times. Few exist now a day, due to the lack of emphasis being places on these skills.

For me, Finishing/Charm School was a defining moment in my life, and the best thing my parents could have done for their socially inept, awkward, low self-esteem, depressed, shy daughter. At the time, I didn't feel like I had a choice, I wasn't angry about it, however I felt they were forcing me to go.

Since my mom had been sick for the last few years, I was much closer to my dad and went to him when I had a question, problem or wanted permission to do something. He had been concerned about my depression even though we never called it that in those days. I knew he wanted the best for me. I was a Daddy's Girl and I still wanted to please him, so if he wanted me to go to this school then I was going to go.

First days were still hard and painful for me, so I turned on my invisible mode and decided to just try my best to get through the day. I remember getting dressed that first morning.

What to wear?? I changed my dress four times.

Which shoes? Black, of course.

Purse? I only had one purse that I packed full of everything I thought I'd need for the day.

As I was driving downtown on my way to the orientation

class, my anxiety was high as I hadn't driven in a lot of traffic or been downtown much. I was stressed and started talking out loud to myself;

"Where do I park?

"I hope I don't have to try and parallel park. No, I'll have to drive around the block because I can't. Dang!"

"So many cars and traffic lights. Yikes!"

"I hope there aren't any steep hills, I'm still learning to drive and shift gears. UGH!!"

"Maybe I should just go back home."

"Why did I think I could do this?"

"Nope, I can't go home . . . I just have to get through the first day."

By the time I parked and found the building I was full of anxiety and fear. I just stood in the lobby, off to the side, for a few minutes and closed my eyes. I was just trying to get my heart to slow down and prepare myself to walk into the classroom that morning.

I took that last big breath as I turned the door handle and it was like I was stepping off a cliff as I walked into the room looking around. I was greeted immediately by one of the instructors, who shook my hand and introduced herself, welcoming me to the first day. I didn't realize I was holding my breath until it came out on a whoosh.

She was a tall, blond, perfectly styled, hair in a French twist, looking cool, calm, and comfortable. She has an easy smile as she held my hand a couple of seconds longer giving me a light squeeze and a chance to breathe again before she turned and introduced me to the others.

In that moment I knew I was going to be all right. The other young women were like me; scared, timid, shy and there because their parents sent them, trying to make the best of a stressful situation. There were 8 of us and I had found my tribe.

Our instructors were wise women who were experienced in training the awkward and insecure; giving us skills to become confidant, assured young women. They had a whole year to mold, encourage, prod and provide us with new habits, tools and techniques.

Our days were split in half. Mornings were all about posture, presence, etiquette, walking, talking, manners, self-esteem, image management, etc. I remember one of our beginning posture lessons was learning how to walk properly on a runway. The classroom had the runway down the middle of the room and we were being taught how to sit with our ankles crossed, never our knees.

The instructor was telling us, "Ladies never cross their knees, always sit up straight, legs together, bent slightly to the right or left side and one ankle crossed lightly over the other." As we were practicing standing and sitting, I misjudged where the chair was and slid off it onto the floor.

I sat there in shock...

Before I could scramble up the instructor stopped me. As she was standing above me in her black suit and crisp white blouse looking poised and confident, there were a few giggles and I was mortified. I lowered my head and closed my eyes, she immediately leaned over, lifted my chin, looked me in the eyes and said, "Ladies never cower or giggle at other's misfortune and this is how you gracefully rise from an unexpected mishap." She then had us all practice getting up off the floor, as she informed us someday this would happen to everyone in the room and we must be prepared.

Every day was a learning lesson of some sort. Little by little my confidence and self-esteem grew. I was much more comfortable with myself and had fewer and fewer episodes of depression. I was enjoying the classes and feeling of belonging. I was less and less afraid of meeting new people or going new places. I was enjoying going out dancing with my friends on the weekend to the point that I was confident enough to go by myself after work to meet up with friends. Something that wasn't even a consideration the year before.

I remember one evening leaving work and heading to a dance club. I had been to it before and that night I went without knowing if anyone I knew would be there or not. I had to park a couple of blocks away and as I was walking to the club I was laughing to myself, thinking how much I had changed in the last year. I had been looking forward to going out all during my shift and there was no fear only excited anticipation.

It felt awesome.

I remember walking in, the music was blaring and I went straight to the dance floor. I had so much fun that night and it was a magical evening for me as I celebrated my growth and how happy I was at that moment.

Classes continued with Etiquette being a large part of our daily lessons; learning everything from the proper usage of silverware in a formal setting to the correct way to enter and leave a room. There were many sessions on hair, makeup and choice of clothing. We learned different modeling techniques and the use of the runway and unstructured types of modeling events. By the end of the year, we started participating in local fashion shows for the experience and training. It was frightening and exhilarating at the same time.

I remember my first restaurant fashion show was during the lunch hour. I was very nervous and didn't know exactly what to expect. We had practiced in a dining room setting, without anyone else in the room, but us. Walking among the tables and spinning was going to be tricky.

I didn't actually remember my first pass through the room, as I was too busy thinking of all the things to remember. Keep my head up, back straight, walk slowly, smile, spin twice in the room, then had to change before my second round. While changing my outfit, I was reminded to not be so stiff, to smile more and to look at a couple of the diners.

The second time was a little easier walking among the round tables, until I actually tried to look at someone, when he smiled back at me I froze for a moment then remembered where I was, blushed and moved on. I did notice that time, that most of the diners were businessmen eating their lunch while we modeled around their tables.

I hadn't been that close to someone when I had modeled before, so it was a little distracting and made me uncomfortable and self-conscious. By the third round I knew what to expect and I walked that room like I owned it.

Afternoons were classroom-type settings and the interior design course. It was interesting, as we learned about the history of the clothing industry, advertising, furniture designs, etc. We visited museums, attended decorating shows and listened to designers. I especially remember my group going to the Hearst Castle, in San Simeon, California.

Hearst Castle is a national historical site full of architectural designs and opulent furniture from around the world. The mansion sits up on the hill overlooking the Pacific Ocean, on 127 acres of gardens, terraces and pools. The view is breathtaking.

On our drive up the coast that morning, we were in a 12-passenger van that was noisy with all us girls talking and giggling. We had been on day excursions before, however this was the first time we were staying overnight in a hotel and our energy was high.

As we pulled up the long driveway, we were all trying to get a good look at the front of the castle. Our faces were pressed up to the windows as we tried to get our first looks at it. The mansion was magnificent. The front door looked like something from a cathedral and must have been 20 feet tall. All I could see were big columns, lots of windows, everything intricately carved with statues and beautiful landscaping and that was just the front entrance.

Once inside it was almost overwhelming. Every room was packed with furniture, art, wall hanging, statues, tables, with lights in every corner, displaying millions of trinkets. The walls were covered with all these incredible portraits, pictures and art of any form imaginable. We were told it was W.R. Hearst's European and Mediterranean art collection.

I loved the old wood and enormous pieces of furniture that were beautifully carved and took up whole rooms. The walls and trim were all in stunning old wood carved and embellished in so many different ways. There were huge beams going across the ceilings that were either decorated with more carved wood or had these glorious painted scenes that made me dizzy as I looked up at them.

I was actually relieved once we went outside from all the rooms that were literally stuff with so much of everything that my mind and body had felt over stimulated. That's when we came to my favorite area, the Neptune Pool. It looked like something out of an ancient, mythological setting. There were Greek columns on each end with sitting areas. The bottom of the pool was made of thousands of marble tile pieces in this intricate pattern that was stunningly reflected through the blue water creating this magical space. The King Neptune statue sat at one end of the pool to complete the setting. There were big, comfortable lounging areas around the pool and the view was breathtaking of the gardens overlooking the Pacific Ocean in the background. As I stood there that afternoon I was in awe of all the beauty before my eyes.

The day was full of so many examples I had only studied in books and now I was actually seeing them in person. It was a day full of magic and wonder and opulence and grandeur. At dinner that night we all couldn't stop talking about all things each of us had seen that day. It was a wonderful end to a magical day and one I look back on with fond memories.

###

Now to be honest, I didn't know what WOO was until recently. WOO is the acronym for Winning Others Over. This is one of my strengths identified in Gallup's program called Strengths Finders. This is an on-line site that has a large list of questions that takes about 30 minute to answer the random questions. Depending on your combined answer it gives you your top five strengths and several pages of information on each one.

I had never heard of WOO before I took this test or that it was considered a strength. I just knew that once I felt comfortable on how to enter a room, use eye contact, shake hands, make small talk, ask questions and connect, I thoroughly enjoyed the process. My WOO really began to blossom after I finished Charm School.

After my year, I had more confidence and did some more modeling, yet didn't feel drawn to pursue it or the design field. My first few jobs were as a waitress and in retail sales. I became pretty good at both, mainly because I had found a way to enjoy meeting people and I was approachable. I learned to take the time and ask questions. Waitressing was easy for me and I made great tips, just because I was friendly and could interact with my customers. My years of observing and studying human nature provided me with a wealth of knowledge to draw from.

My all-time favorite waitressing job was at Oscar's Restaurant. It was a 24-hour diner with rollers skating, drive-up carhops. No, that was not my job, as I was never coordinated enough to roller skate and carry a tray and I knew my limitations. I worked the 8pm to 4am shift that summer, inside the diner. I loved that shift, as it gave me so much freedom with my day consisting of usually getting home by 5am, sleeping until noonish, getting up, eating, then going to the beach all afternoon until early evening, running home, in just enough time to get a shower and head to work by 8pm.

I remember one Friday night I arrived a little early, even though I had been at the beach all day and I was in a great mood. It was a beautiful, summer evening and lots of people were out. Oscar's was the place to hang out that summer. As I came onto the floor for my shift, the place was buzzing with activity. Several families were having dinner and a group of new friends I had made that summer were hanging out waiting for me.

The Beach Boys were playing on the jukebox, as I jumped in and started taking orders, laughing and getting my hugs. The dinner shift flew by and soon my parents were coming in the door with, Aunt Bonnie and Uncle Jim and some their friends after bowling to visit and get something to eat.

I had been bringing home my new friends I had met that summer, so my parents knew them and it became one big, reunion in my section. Then my brother Steve showed up with his high school buddies, plus a few of my friends making it full blown party at Oscar's that evening. It eventually rolled over to the parking lot and I remember standing there at one point hardly able to contain my joy and excitement at how much fun I was having.

My parents left about midnight and my friends were coming and going. I kept working through my shift stopping to greet and get hugs from the people there that night. By 2am, we were busy again as the bars closed down and people wanted something to eat before going home.

The night just flew by and as I was cleaning up and ending my shift, a friend I mine stopped by and asked if I wanted to go to the beach and watch the sun rise. Why not?? It was 4am and I was stilled wired from my shift and knew I wouldn't be able to sleep for a while. I jumped in my 1960, brown, Corvair and drove to the beach. We walked, talked and watched the sun rise. Best day ever. I went home, slept, went back to the beach and then to work that night. Perfect summer!!

###

What I have learned about WOO is my need to get others to like me, Winning Others Over. Strangers weren't intimidating any more, in fact, they energized me and I wanted to find more. The more people I could meet and learn their stories, the happier I was. I basically didn't know any strangers, just people I hadn't met yet. This is still my favorite thing about networking, traveling, socializing, etc. -- whom I get to meet next.

I have met so many interesting people, had some of my most intense conversations, solved many of the world's problems and made lots of new friends by this need to find out their story. It truly has become something that gets me excited, engaged and my adrenaline running. Even when I don't actually connect with someone it's the whole process that keeps me trying different ways.

I actually had to laugh at myself a couple of years ago, when I just couldn't connect with this person I met at a networking event. This was not long after I discovered what WOO was and how I used it for me. When I attend any kind of event, even home parties, I always look around for the people standing by themselves. I'm drawn to them, mostly because of my past and I remember how hard it was for me to approach others, so I try and make it easy for them.

This event was at a restaurant/ bar and when I walked in there was a man sitting at the bar by himself, watching everyone else, but not socializing at all. After I circled the room, he was still alone, so I walked over and introduced myself. I tried for several minutes to start a conversation with him and he was generally unresponsive or one word answers, so I moved on.

Now here's the funny part, it bothered me that I couldn't connect, so I actually went back twice to try again to find something we could talk about. Finally he told me that he wasn't there to talk to anyone, that he came to this bar after work each day to unwind and didn't like all these people invading his space.

I apologized and walked away laughing at myself, as that was my WOO in full gear. I was just not going to give up and he became like a challenge that I needed to convince and win over. This was definitely a life lesson for me that night and something I am much more aware of these days; that it's not a competition and to let go and move on when others don't want to engage. It's really okay and life is much easier and more fun for me now.

Trust me, over the years I have found there are certain personalities and others strengths that I don't mesh with and have learned to steer clear of them. I've even worked with a few that made the work environment difficult and so unbearable that going back each day was uncomfortable for us all. I had some great managers that paid attention and handled the situations and I've had a couple that ignored the issues and allowed us to wallow in it.

If things became unbearable, I always chose to move on and find myself another position with a better environment, rather than stay and try to continue to mix oil and water. We cannot make all people happy and I can only take care of my own happiness not that of others. Luckily, this has not happened very often in my lifetime, but when I was in the middle of it and even my WOO couldn't make it better, no matter what I tried, I moved on where my skills and WOO were appreciated. Life is too short to stay in positions and situations that at the end of the day you are miserable and hate going back the next day. Be kind to yourself and make a change as you are worth it and deserve your own kind of happy ending.

My Advice to You:

If you're not a natural WOOer (doesn't that sound like a Dr. Seuss character?), find someone who is and be his or her friend. You see them every day. They're the ones laughing, always talking, and asking questions, with lots of energy. Hang out with them, network where they do, go where they go, take them to coffee or lunch. Most WOOers love helping other people. Tell them what you want and learn. Then go out and WOO to your heart's content. It'll never hurt, and you could learn to love it.

In addition, maybe Finishing Schools should make a comeback. I actually looked them up on-line and a few of these schools still exist. I think we need to place more emphasis on Social and Business Etiquette, Image Development, Posture and Presence, Presentation Skills, Health and Self-Esteem, etc.? Every day I see inappropriate behavior from unsuspecting individuals who have no idea how they appear to others.

We learn these skills from our family, friends, peers, co-workers, bosses; then schools, play grounds, offices, social and public events. We are all products of our environments and the people in them; which are not all positive, healthy atmospheres or role models. As a society, there is more emphasis placed on what we have materialistically than on our social and business skills and graces. Our success is judged by our material possessions and not how we treat people.

Social media is a wonderful tool; however, we now have a society that spends more time on their mobile devices than actually having conversations. We have a rule in our family. . . No phones at the dinner table. For that period of time we can listen and share. So put down your phones, close your laptops and shut your computers off regularly, then find someone to talk to, live, love and be present.

Janet Ravenscraft

CHAPTER 4
QUIET OBSERVER ON BULLYING

"Sometimes it's the quiet observer that sees the most."
~Kathryn L. Nelson

In the next few years, I found many ways to use my WOO; however, there were still times that I'd revert to being invisible rather than just observing, depending on the situation, who I was with and my attitude. I was pretty good at using what worked best for me.

Since I spent a number of years watching others and being as quiet and inconspicuous as possible, people didn't usually notice I was around. I've seen all types of behaviors good and bad and even though these behaviors may not have been directed at me I learned from them.

For example, I was drawn to and trusted those who were kind to animals. If I was around someone who mistreated, bullied or even just teased their pets I stayed away from them. Animals have an innate sense of who can be trusted, especially if someone is aggressive or unkind and I learned that same skill. As children, we see much more than adults give us credit for and most of those observations are how we learn to treat others and set up our own boundaries in life.

In my observations, we are all products of our environments and how we interact at home with siblings, parents, relatives and extended family members doesn't always work well in social arenas. I don't know about your house, but with my brothers there was a lot of yelling, teasing, screaming, fighting, arguing, etc., that went on in my home and those of my relatives. We weren't always nice to each other, yet we were loyal and protective if someone else tried to hurt or be mean to any of us.

Teasing and tattling are not skills that work well in most work environments or relationships, yet that's what happens in a lot of family settings. Usually the oldest or the youngest, whoever was the loudest, got the most attention. We all learned how to irritate or push our siblings and parents over the edge with a look or a word. As we learned how we fit in our own families we brought those skills with us as we went out in the world.

Next, School taught us about groups and cliques, popular kids and the rest of us, and survival of the fittest. We copied how people treated each other, depending on our personalities, and adopted what worked best for us. Many recreated how they were treated at home for how they treated others. If you we're picked on and bullied at home it often rolled over into your behavior in school. If you were nurtured and told you could do or be anything you believed it and encouraged others.

Then we get our first job, and learn more habits of good and bad ways to interact with others and get along. Unfortunately, there are bad bosses out there, and this ends up reinforcing a family's and/or a school's bad behavior. This is the only foundation for some, who wonder why they don't have very many friends or why they can't get, keep or move up in their lives and jobs. It can be a vicious circle.

I saw this in my youngest brother John, who, when he was little, was small for his age and an easy target with a short temper and fuse. His older brother, Steve, was laid back, easy going and could just look at him in a certain way and my younger brother would be immediately angry and defensive.

Many a battle was had by the two of them growing up and no words were ever exchanged. Sometimes they'd just look at each other and start wrestling and pounding on each other. Steve usually had the height advantage, until John became faster and more aggressive. Steve had a way, like most brothers of knowing what buttons to push with just a little smirk or laugh and John would go ballistic and attack.

The neighborhood boys helped reinforce his temper by not letting him play with them or telling him to close his eyes and count to 10, and then he'd have to find them. Instead of hiding they'd take off and leave him looking for them. He'd get so mad when he figured it out and stomp home yelling all the way calling them names.

So by the time he went to school he already had a chip on his shoulder and learned to pick fights first, using what he called the element of surprise. He carried that "everybody's picking on me" attitude throughout his life and used it often to explain why things didn't go his way. Lucky for him, he was also a charmer and had a quirky sense of humor that often helped him talk himself out of situations.

I remember one day when he was about 8 years old, coming home with a bloody nose and being so proud of himself for getting in a fight because the other kids told him he was too little to play with them. He stood there with his bloody nose and his hands on his hips telling my mom the story, that he went up to the biggest kid and tackled him. They scuffled until the other boys pulled them apart and told him if he was mean enough to start a fight, they wanted him on their team and he could play with them from now on.

From that day forward, this was how he behaved so he could be included and solved his tendency to be bullied by other. Bully the bully. Just watching him grow up and remembering all the situations he got himself into is why I believe bullies still exist in workplaces, homes and social environments. These skills are learned at young ages in homes and on the playgrounds.

My youngest brother John was a tortured soul with a heart of gold who was bullied when he was young and throughout his life. His edgy personality and sometime sketchy behavior didn't win him a lot of friends. I believe to this day that if he had been treated with more kindness and acceptance he may have felt like he didn't have to fight first.

By the time he had been diagnosed with Bi-Polar, his body had deteriorated beyond recovery. In his last few years, he was very kind, loving and had this wicked sense of humor that you couldn't help but laugh with him. Because of him I will not allow the weak or the meek to be bullied or made to feel bad about themselves. Every Body Matters and I want to be the Love.

My bullying was more in the form of not being good enough. This was most evident whenever groups had to be divided up into "teams". There are all types of situations where "teams" are created; neighborhoods, backyard, playgrounds, schools, work, family get-togethers, etc. Most are sports related, however even family game night, workshops and any kind of competitions that break into groups the weak are picked last.

I've established that I wasn't the most coordinated or

aggressive person, so when others were forced to include me the heavy signs, frowns and just being the last person picked left me feeling like I was not good enough. My least favorite playground game ever was "Red Rover, Red Rover Send Janet Over".

If you've never played this game, here's how it works. The group is split up into two teams. Picking captains, and then selecting one person at a time. Teams lined up facing each other holding hands. During the game, each team picks someone from the other team to run and try to break through the opposite line, picking the presumed weakest on the other team to eliminate him or her.

I remember the rejected feeling of being picked last and told to go to the end of the line as the weakest link. I'd hear things like, "She'll never break through." "She needs to be on the end, because she can't stop anyone." Then I was usually the first one picked from my team to try and break through the other team's line. The groans and complaints that, "She can't do it." from my own team were so hurtful and unkind and just added more pressure and stress to my own timidity.

I don't remember any words of encouragement only lots of yelling like "Hurry up", "You can't do it" and "Come on we don't have all day". That non-aggressive part of me had no desire to run at the other line, but I couldn't walk away or just stand there and be called a quitter or baby. That was way worse than just being yelled at and pushed around, so I'd closed my eyes and run. The sad part is I don't remember ever breaking through any of those lines. All that did was reinforce the "I must not be good enough, if I can't even break through the Red Rover line." I never liked the game or the outcome of being the first to be eliminated and the jeers and complaints from my own teammates.

###

I saw enough of bullying around me, yet I'd never felt strong or confident enough to do anything about it. I remember playing in the neighborhood with the other kids when I was about eight. We'd play Kick the Can most evenings from dusk until dark, when the streetlights came on. It was summer, so we'd played until usually 10:00 at night. There were about a dozen of us, including my three cousins who lived around the corner from us. We'd all meet in the middle and our version was the person who was 'It' had to tag someone else before they Kicked the Can. Once tagged, you were 'It.'

One of the neighborhood boys who played with us was a bully who picked on the smaller, weaker and timid boys, usually leaving us girls alone, because he knew our older male cousin would protect us. However, there were a couple of younger boys that were his targets. He would yell at them and call them babies or chase only them until he could grab or push them down. I was afraid for them and could tell how afraid or mad they would get as they picked themselves up off the ground. It would make me feel sad and helpless that I never tried to stop it from happening or had the courage to say something to the bully.

I was still in that mode of doing everything possible to not be noticed and bring any attention to myself. I learned to steer away from those that bullied others and felt like the "Chicken" the bully was picking on, as I snuck away. In any type of competition or situation that I felt might lead to me being bullied, I'd create some imaginary injury or lag back long enough that the games had already begun. This way I could observe and not be what I considered on the firing line.

I saw a different kind of bullying after I joined the Air Force. Yes, I was in the Air Force. Not what you thought I was going to say, huh? I was at a crossroads in my young life and still didn't know what I wanted to do. Charms schools had given me the confidence in myself, while food service and sales had given me the work ethic and business skills. Yet, I still wanted more and I really wanted to get out of town and see the world. The problem was I didn't know where to go and didn't have a lot of money or the courage to just take off and see where life took me.

A number of incidents lead me to decide to join the Air Force that summer. There was so much unrest in our country, regarding the Vietnam War that had started in 1954. This war was still going on in 1969, the year I graduated from high and also the year the Draft Lottery was implemented again. All young men born from 1944 to 1950 were required to sign up for the draft lottery when they turned 18.

My "Perfect Summer" was towards the end of the Vietnam War and many of my friends had been drafted into the Army or had been forced to join other branches of the military, otherwise they'd be sent to the frontline.

Protestors were just another kind of bully. They believed the war was wrong and we shouldn't have troops there, so they started large protests and riots in cities and on college campuses across the nation. Draft card and public burning of the American flag were commonplace. Young men were leaving the country to avoid the draft and refused to join the military.

During this time, as soldiers were returning from tours of duty in Vietnam they were struggling with readjusting to a country that didn't appreciate their services or sacrifices. They were not welcomed back into the United States as war heroes like they are now, they were scorned, ridiculed, attacked and took the brunt of the countries anger and frustration.

I realized the American people who were against the war, were bullying the Vietnam soldiers who were lucky enough to survive and come home. They had been fighting for their lives in a hostile country far away and as they came home they were being condemned and made to feel like no cared about them or the many who had lost their lives or been maimed.

But as the daughter of a Navy sailor, I saw the long hours and months that my dad was away from his family to protect the freedoms everyone took for granted and it made me angry. I didn't understand the disrespect that was aimed at him and those that were fighting the actual war, as they weren't making the decisions yet it felt like they were getting all the blame.

By this time, my dad had already served one tour in Vietnam on board an aircraft carrier that provided the jets for the air attacks. He had joined the military at the end of the Korean War and had been in when the Vietnam War started in 1954. He was a true patriot who believes he served to protect the freedoms of our country.

I remember the day "Hanoi" Jane Fonda protested outside the base where my dad was stationed. She was a public bully, who used her notoriety to organize a protest that morning. The protestors blocked the way for the sailors to get on base and report to their ships for duty that morning. My dad came home that day so angry and frustrated telling us the protestor's numbers had grown to a huge group that day.

He said as each car was trying to drive on base, the protestors were banging on the hoods and windows yelling at every sailor trying to go to work. He said he could see their angry, distorted faces, pressed up against his car windows, in front and all around his car. Some were leaning on the hood with signs protesting the war and he could hear the protestors yelling things like "baby killer" "war monger" "killing machines". He was so distraught about some of the awful things they were yelling that he wouldn't even repeat them. He told us as he finally inched his way to the front gate, there was Jane Fonda on a bullhorn, standing on top of a car, riling everyone up into a frenzy.

The protestors had disrupted the whole day and everyone had been sent home in intervals and out by different gates and alternate routes to avoid the chaos from the morning and the protestors still there. He was inconsolable that afternoon because he did not understand and felt helpless to do anything about it all. That day made me want to do something to show support for my dad that I believed in him.

The last incident that made me decide to join the military was when I went to visit a friend in the VA hospital. I remember my friend Casey before he went to Vietnam, as a laid back surfer who lived down by the beach. Easy going, kind and fun to hang out with. He was drafted when he was 18 and when he came back at 20, he had been injured and was in the VA hospital recovery from his surgeries.

As I walked through the hospital that day, I was shocked by all the young guys with missing limbs, eyes, bandages everywhere, burns and injuries that I couldn't even see, but knew existed. I saw so many sad eyes and the worst ones were vacant, like no one was there. I had never been around that many people who had suffered things I couldn't even imagine in a million years. I was deeply affected by all the soldiers there who were broken, lost and some beyond repair. I couldn't take it all in.

By the time I found Casey, my mind was numb and it took everything I had that day to hold it together. Casey was no longer the carefree surfer I had known. Physically he had recovered from his injuries, but had lost so much weight, his face was gaunt and his clothes were baggy. Mentally he was a wreck and heavily medicated that day due to the horrific nightmares he had been experiencing. He was rambling and delusional not really having a conversation with me, more with himself.

I left that afternoon and wandered around for several hours, my mind just going over every detail of my visit to the hospital. The sadness was so overwhelming I couldn't even cry. I decided I wanted to be a nurse. My empathetic side kicked into overdrive and I was going to figure out a way to save them all.

By the next day, reality set in and I decided the best way to get the training was to enlist myself. I talked to my parents about it and though they were surprised they didn't try and talk me out of it. My dad suggested I go and talk to a couple of recruiters, but that he didn't really want me to join the Army and actually end up in Vietnam. He felt I could be just as much help here in the states and still get a good education and training.

I did as he suggested and took the test to determine what fields I would qualify for, yet still determined to get into nursing. In the infinite wisdom of the Universe taking care of me, I was not enrolled in the nursing program and know to this day I would have never made a good nurse. Divine intervention kept me from a career that would have destroyed me, especially if I had tried to go into trauma care. I am too soft hearted, can hardly stand the site of blood and can't even imagine having to try and draw blood or give someone a shot, no less all the other requirements of that noble profession.

What I was good at were organizational and administrative skills and I have a high mechanical ability, so I ended up in the Air Force, stationed at Ellsworth Air Force base, in Rapid City, South Dakota. I was assigned to a Parts and Repair center keeping track of missile parts as they were removed and replaced.

As for the military, they have what some consider their own type of bullying, called the military way. I don't know of another way to train large groups to listen, not argue, and follow orders, with no questions asked. The men were all being trained for combat and their lives and the lives of others depended on complete obedience.

In the beginning, basic training is to bring all the young recruits together and begin to teach everyone, one way; the military way. For me it wasn't as difficult as it was for those not from military families. I was brought up to respect authority and my elders, I knew how to follow order and directions without questioning why or just choose not to do what I was told.

I was selected as one of four squad leaders in my barracks and became a leader that first week. I taught my squad to march, pass inspections, memorize code, take test, do laundry, follow orders and sing a lot of cadence, the military way.

Did we get yelled at? Sure did. Were we reprimanded when we screwed up? You betcha. Did we all learn to wake up at 5:00am, make our beds, get dressed in record time, march to breakfast in the dark, eat quickly, march to class in double time, not fall asleep in class, march and do drills every afternoon, march to get shots weekly, and just march, march, march? "Yes, Sir, Master Sargent, Yes, Sir."

It was the military, with a chain of command, we were taught not to question, comment, complain or talk back. All were unacceptable and caused immediate negative consequences; that could include the whole unit being reprimanded, if one soldier chose not follow orders. It was the military and if you expected something else you were released and sent home regardless of the branch of the service. If you didn't follow orders, you weren't asked nicely. You knew what they were and if you chose not to do them then you were punished accordingly. Some consider this bullying. I accept it for what it is; a proven training tool to ensure obedience.

Only men were being prepared for real life combat. At that time, women were not allowed to be on the frontlines or in combat positions. Only in the last decade those restrictions have been lifted. Women did not go through the obstacle or artillery training courses as part of basic training.

For the combat training, those in command only wanted soldiers who understood the importance of the rules and could be depended to do what they were told. In combat, other people's lives depended on everyone working together at that moment, not stopping to explain themselves, just do as you're told. So call it bullying if you want; however the military has survived all these years because of those rules and regulations being followed by the masses. I'm glad the mandatory draft hasn't been necessary since Vietnam, as it created so much turmoil and issues for all concerned.

My Advice to You:

Do not tolerate bullying of any kind.

I am encouraged that "Bullying" is finally being addressed in society as a whole, even though bullies still run companies, offices, sports programs, playgrounds and families. Bullying still happens in our homes, schools and work environments. More is being done to discourage it, as companies, schools and churches create programs to address the issues and help those being bullied. I truly hope that all the emphasis being placed on how destructive bullying is and the lack of tolerance society is willing to accept now, will change the way of the world forever.

This is why I support programs like Derrick Boles, "Standup America" and "Stand Beautiful". These programs are addressing the problems of bullying and self-esteem starting at the grade school level for both boys and girls. It imperative that we as adults provide programs and tools for children to learn compassion, tolerance and the confidence to stop bullying. That every child knows that they are perfect just the way they are. See the Resources section for more information on these program and ones like them.

There are still times I craved anonymity, when I just want to be an observer. I learned so much by just watching other people--how they interact, how they treat each other, what works for them, what doesn't. It's still a tool I use often and even purposefully to just people-watch.

As an observer, I have improved my listening skills over the years. I've noticed that people have a hard time listening, as they are spending all their energy preparing their responses. It's especially apparent when they keep interrupting and wanting to insert their two cents before the person has finished their thought.

There were many times when I didn't think anyone wanted to hear what I had to say anyway or I didn't know what to add to a conversation, so I would just sit, listen and watch everyone else. I have learn a number of different techniques that show the person you are having a conversation with that you are interested in what they are saying and that you are listening.

Here are a few: Always look them in the eye and find something nice to say about their appearance, eyes, smile, jewelry, clothing, anything personal showing them you are aware of them. Don't keep looking around the room to see who else is there or checking your phone to see what you're missing. Give that person your undivided attention for the time you are together. Be Present.

Connect in some way by shaking hands or touching their sleeve while you are complimenting them on something you have observed about them. Be genuine and use those moments to find a common ground, even if it's just how wonderful or not the weather has been that day.

The art of small talk seems to be decreasing as everyone is so connected electronically and by social media that we don't seem to take the time and just have good, old, fashion conversations. There is a lot of talk about how life is so short, yet we don't seem to be taking advantage of improving our verbal skills.

I remember one time when a couple of very good friends of mine were picking me up at the airport. When they walked up, I was saying goodbye and hugging this woman. They asked me who she was, and how I knew her, since we were so friendly. I told them, "Oh, I just met her an hour ago on our flight, and we had this great conversation." They just started shaking their heads and commented, "Of course you just met her and what probably had a past life together." Even though I had known these friends for a while, they were still surprised that we were hugging like long-lost best friends. I just couldn't help myself and told my friends aren't we the lucky ones we get to be friends all the time.

CHAPTER 5
INQUISITIVE - FINDING THE ANSWERS

"There is nothing that can help you understand your beliefs more than trying to explain them to an inquisitive child."
~Frank A. Clark

All of my life I have been inquisitive. Even when I was invisible, I was inquisitive. You know those kids whose minds you can see working as they try to figure out how something works or how to do something? I didn't always feel comfortable asking "why" or "what if," but I definitely didn't have a problem with touching it, taking it apart, or studying it.

I remember as a young child standing in front of the stove and my mom telling me, "Don't touch that . . . hot!" I was looking up at the blue and yellow flames and thinking they're so pretty and they look so soft. My brain didn't really know what hot was and I really wanted to still touch it. Up my little hand went towards the flame, reaching as far as I could, just as I was starting to feel what hot was, my mom grabbed my hand. She crouched down in front of me my holding my hand and said, "See that's hot and will burn you, don't touch."

Ouch, now that made sense.

I'm a visual, tactile/touchy-feely kind of person. I need to see and feel how things work for my brain to fully understand. I wasn't necessarily defiant; I just couldn't let it go until I knew the how and what.

In elementary school, when we were first learning to count, we used beans. This was perfect for me, because I could touch and see the beans and the numbers increase or decrease as I added or took away beans. I remember being worried, "What was I going to use when I didn't have beans to count." As I observed some of the other kids using their fingers, I was excited to have a backup plan and started using my fingers, too. I was always trying to stay one step ahead, figuring out what I needed next, so I wouldn't have to actually ask someone.

As I grew up and couldn't figure things out on my own,
I eventually learned how to ask questions. Sometimes I asked too many questions that could be annoying, confusing or irritating for others. My family, friends and coworkers didn't always appreciate my inquisitiveness. People will humor you when you're a child for only so long before they tell you, "Because I said so."

Once when I was a teenager, I wanted to know how a plane flew in the air. My dad and I were standing in the front yard for over 30 minutes, as I asked him questions like, "How does it go up?" What makes it stay in the air?" "How does thrust get all that weight off the ground?" "What do you mean the wings are built to balance the weight?" "Wings can't be built that big!" "I just don't get it." "Whose mind is set up like that to figure that kind of stuff out? "And so on. Luckily for me, my dad had a lot of patience and could usually handle my questions and persistence.

After a half an hour my dad told me he had to get some

yard work done. I followed him around for a while and kept trying to ask the same questions over and over again in a different way and he kept working and repeating his answers. I finally gave up and went in the house. Seriously planes flying in the sky still boggle my mind to this day.

###

As my younger self with WOO, there were times when I could still annoy people with my questions. I eventually learned to curb or hold my questions when I was around someone who I could tell was getting frustrated with my inquisitiveness and me.

I have created one of those bigger than life personalities that can seriously just get away from me some times. I also have a loud, strong voice that carries and an infectious laugh that identifies me and makes it easy for my family to find me. When I get wound up and excited about something, it can seriously be too much for some people.

One time when a manager was trying to explain how a new software program was going to be used, I kept asking questions that he couldn't answer. I was excited about the program and what I thought it was going to be able to provide and peppered him with questions. Finally he put his hands up and told me to go talk to the programmer.

Now conversations with the programmers aren't much easier. They have their own language, are very linier, and everything is black and white, by code. I'm more all over the place and strategically trying to work out problems and questions in my head as I go along. My question was something like, "I see steps 1 and 4, but how do we get 2 and 3? His response, "I wrote it just as requested. There was no 2 or 3." Me, "Well we need 2 and 3, we can't go from 1 to 4." Him, "That should have been in the original specs, now I have to rewrite it." Me, "Okay let's try this again, I apologize we didn't provide all the data up front. What do you need from us? Learning to ask the correct questions and knowing what to provide in the beginning was another lesson learned.

Parties and celebration are where I really like to shine, when people are happy and wanting to have fun. I like to get people dancing and involved in the gaiety, as often people want to be part of it all, but just don't know how to start or be the first. I want to talk to everyone there. I reacquaint myself with old friends or relative and can't wait to meet those I don't know. I've been asked to join other people's celebrations just because I was having more fun than they were at their gathering.

This is the truth, I was once out with a small group of women and we were having so much fun, laughing and dancing and interacting with everyone. I kept asking everyone we met questions, like "Where are you from?" "What's your favorite color?" "What are you celebrating tonight?" Just random questions, as I was getting to know all these new people, then I would just invite them to join us. We eventually ended up with well over a dozen of us all together. People and couples started hanging out with us and when we moved to another establishment they moved with us. By the end of the evening, we were all new best friends and exchanged phone numbers and made arrangements to get together again. That's what I like to do as I used my inquisitiveness to meet new people and make new friendships.

When I was in the Air Force, being inquisitive was an asset and appreciated as a strength of mine. Never questioned authority, as that was a no, no, however making sure I had all the critical information needed to complete a project or utilizing my attention to detail to obtain all the necessary information were skills I used daily. Sometimes others need to be prodded to get all the information required for me to complete my side of a job.

A perfect example was when I would take parts in for repair. I couldn't just write down broken, as the repair unit would send it back requiring more information. I would then have to track down the person who removed the part and ask a number of questions to find out the exact problem, before I returned it to the repair unit. I was good at this side of my job, because I knew how to keep asking questions in different ways until I could get the full picture. My attention to detail was a necessity to keep the shop running in an orderly fashion.

I enjoyed my time in the Air Force. It wasn't difficult for me. I had no trouble with basic training or tech school. In three months I had done my basic training in Texas, gone to Denver for my technical training, then stationed in South Dakota. The hard part for me was going from living in lovely, warm California to freezing, cold South Dakota. Even though I had lived on the East Coast until I was 12, it had been many years since I had experienced long, cold winters. That first winter was brutal.

I was issued a parka and moon boots the first day I arrived in South Dakota and not a moment too soon. When I was a kid and it got below zero outside, we just weren't allowed out of the house. Quite different when you have to go to work, in December, on the flight line and your office is in a hanger.

Cold had a whole new meaning and that first winter I ended up with frostbite on my fingers and toes. It happened one day when I walked over to the PX and Chow Hall by myself, to shop for a few items and get some lunch. It was my day off and since I had been there only a couple of weeks I wanted to see what this base had to offer. The sun was shining, so I grabbed my coat and headed out.

All was good until I came out and realized it had started snowing. Dang, I didn't have my hat, but I did find my little knit gloves in my pocket, pulled them on, grabbed my bags and headed back to the barracks. It was only about a mile, so I wasn't too worried. After a couple of minutes, it wasn't just snowing any more, it was blowing sideways, straight at me and I could only see a couple few feet in front of me. I turned around and couldn't see the PX building anymore either, so I put my head down; leaned forward and stayed on what I thought was the sidewalk. I not only didn't have a hat, but my cute, little, blue street shoes were no match for the ice and freezing cold temperatures and neither were my little, knit gloves. By the time I fell into the barracks, I couldn't feel my feet and fingers.

Everyone in the dayroom scramble to help me that afternoon, as the storm raged on outside, inside it was orderly chaos. This wasn't their first snowstorm or taking care of a rookie who didn't dress properly for the weather. They pulled my jacket, gloves and shoes off and four of them started rubbing my fingers and feet, while someone threw a blanket around my head and shoulders.

My hands and feet burned, ached and tingled as the feeling came back into each of my extremities. It took a good hour before I stopped chattering and a while longer until my fingers and toes felt normal again. I was lucky that day that I wasn't out in the cold any longer and that my only life long side effect has been once my fingers and toes get cold it takes forever to warm them up. Lesson learned that I should have asked more questions before I went out that day and made sure I understood how quickly the weather could change there.

It took me a while to adjust to my new base. In my six-week basic training, we were kept so busy every moment of the day, in our section of the base. We marched everywhere, not really allowed to look around, even "at ease" we didn't talk or relax as we were just always anticipating our next orders. During meals we were in and out and require to sit with our platoons in the chow hall.

Our classroom training and marching drills were separate from the men. There weren't a lot of opportunities to ask questions and it wasn't encouraged, so my observing skills went into overdrive and I watched everything the leaders did. Most of the time we were just trying to get through the day and remember everything we were taught and there was no social time.

In tech school, there were several WAF (Women in the Air Force) platoons and female barracks. This all changed in 1976 when the separate status of women in the air force was abolished and we were accepted into that branch of the armed forces much the same way as men. Until then, they put us together so it didn't feel like we were the only woman personnel there. So, it was all still new and I was learning the military way. I asked lots of questions, so I would know what to do each day. By the end of my 8 weeks training, I had just figured out how to get around the base, to and from classes and the chow hall and back to my barracks and I was transferred again.

I had no idea that there had never been a WAF unit on my new base and that I was the 35th WAF to be stationed there that year. There were only 35 WAF on the whole base and we were all a novelty. It took a little getting used to, being stared at everywhere I went. Since there had never been a WAF unit on that base before and it was some time before people quit staring. I remember the first time I went to chow hall, the other girls warned me it was going to feel strange with so many men around and so few of us. They told me that eating in the chow hall was the worse, as no one really talked to us.

They just stared. When we stepped through the door, it felt like we were on stage, as every head turned and followed us from the door to the

The base was 10 miles from the nearest town and no daily bus service, so unless you had a car you didn't leave the base. The WAF living quarters were one floor of the BAQ (Basic Allowance for Quarters) building. Our floor was more like a college dorms, with two rooms sharing a bathroom in the middle.

We were on the third floor, I guess to keep anyone from climbing in or out of the windows. It coincided with our midnight curfew, which was hard for many of the women even though they told us it as for our protection. We were all over 18 and hadn't joined the service to have a curfew. The doors were locked at midnight and we got demerits if we missed it.

That first winter and during the week, when we all had to work we generally met our curfew, but like anything else when a group feels deprived they find a way to beat the system and we weren't any different. When summer came we found all sorts of crazy ways to sneak out and back, cover for each other, teach the newbies our routine, while we worked and played.

I remember we only had one way in and out through the dayroom and someone was on duty at all times. The other door was an emergency door and if it was opened at any time the alarm would go off and base security would show. We never used that door. If anyone was out late, we'd hang around the dayroom until they came in. We would set watch in case one of our friends were past curfew. Someone would keep watch from a room overlooking the front entrance. Once we'd see her, we'd distract whoever was on duty and sneak our friend in. It wasn't a perfect system, but we did what we could.

I fell in love that summer, hard and fast. John knew who I was before I knew him, as we worked in the same hanger and I sat behind a glass window, which was easier to see into than out of most days. We had both dated other people, so had seen each other but never been introduced.

The day I met him, I was actually in the hospital recovering from bronchitis. It was the end of summer, hot, no air conditioning and I was in a ward with six other women. It was the first day I was actually feeling better and had luckily had my first shower and washed my hair in three days. I'm betting if he had come to see me the day before he would have never asked me out. I was looking and feeling my worse.

That morning when he showed up with another friend of mine, I was sitting cross-legged on my bed trying to tame my thankfully clean hair. I have naturally curly hair that has a mind of its own and every day is an adventure. There were no hair products created yet to tame and manage wild hair, it just was what it was and that day was no exception. Again, at least it was clean. They sat on the floor by my bed while we visited. He brought me the book Clockwork Orange.

I was released back to duty the next day and saw him the following day when he brought some part to have repaired. He told me later it wasn't even his part and that he had taken it from another guy, so he could have a reason to come see me. He asked me if I wanted to go out that weekend and we were a couple from that day forward. I asked a million questions. We talked for hours every day. Being the inquisitive type, no subject was off limits.

We dated for two months and were inseparable. Then I received orders to transfer to Turkey. What?? I didn't want to go and he didn't want me to leave. We talked about it daily for a week and one night, while we were walking back to the barracks, in the middle of the parking lot, he said, "Let's just get married. They won't transfer you if you're married."

I said, "Really you want to get married?" He said, "Sure, we love each other." And that was it. We set a date, called and told our parents, planned a wedding on base at the chapel. One of the girls made my wedding dress. I had a bridal shower and we found a place to live off base. We were married. We met and married in three months.

Some people said "That won't last."

Others said, "She must be pregnant."

Well, we fooled whoever "they" were because we've been married for over 43 years and our first child wasn't born until four years later we were married.

John was up for reenlistment with the Air Force three months after we were married and he chose to leave the military. There were a lot of reasons why we decided to leave then, however most were based on how our country viewed soldiers and military personnel, at that time.

We were not honored or respected by the majority of America. We were uncomfortable wearing our uniforms when we were off base, especially when we traveled or flew anywhere. Some people were cruel and angry over the Vietnam War and took it out on anyone wearing a uniform.

I remember being at an airport in the early 70's waiting for my flight home and watched in horror as some other passengers were harassing two soldiers in fatigues. The soldiers sat for a few minutes with their heads down and never responded as this one man asked them "Do you like killing women and children in those villages?" "How many have you killed?" "I bet you keep track and like it." A couple of others chimed in and were acting like they were disgusted and wouldn't sit next to them.

I was appalled that no one stuck up for them, not even the security guard who just walked by. Then I realized neither did I. I was afraid of what would I be called. I was ashamed that I didn't stand up for them. I didn't know what to do so I did nothing. They just sat with their heads down, until their flight was called and of course, no early boarding for military personnel in those days. I was sick to my stomach the rest of the day and it made me even more leery of telling anyone what I did for a living.

This was during the last couple of years of the war, when tempers were high and the American people were vocal about wanting our country out of Vietnam. Protests were still frequent and violent. There was little pride and it was difficult to want to be in the military. Because of this, John and I decided he would not reenlist and he passed on the reenlistment bonus of $15,000.00 they were offering him. Money didn't matter. He was done hiding and wanted to go back to his life.

Since I was now a married woman, the military rules back then were that my civilian husband had to live within 50 miles of an air base. I would be transferred to that base once they found me a position I was qualified for. It could take up to a year. Hmmm, not the way most people want to start a new marriage. Luckily for me his hometown was further than 50 miles, so I was discharged at the same time.

After the Air Force, John was able to go back to his job with the telephone company, so we moved near his family in Kentucky. We lived there for couple of years while he worked for the telephone company. I took a position in retail sales at a large department store. I was pretty homesick, so after two years I asked John if we could move to San Diego to be near my parents and family. This was just as winter was setting in and he was like, "Let's go." So we quit our jobs, packed everything up in a U-Haul, and moved west.

Once we arrived, we quickly settled in and started looking for new jobs. John got a job working for the school. Debbie, my family friend, cousin by choice and sister from another mister (my dad's best friend Uncle Jim daughter), worked for a local bank and recommended me for a job where she worked. I didn't really want to go back into retail sales, so this was an opportunity to learn something new.

Banks are usually quiet, somber places. I quickly learned people are funny about their money. They can be paranoid, sneaky, stressed and downright mean about it. I had come from the restaurant and retail worlds. They are less strict and more easy-going. I took learning my new duties and fitting in seriously.

I began as a temporary assistant letting people access their safe deposit boxes, filing, counting money and setting up new accounts. I hadn't really worked on a computer before or knew any software programs, so I started from the bottom. New account signature cards were completed on a typewriter, signed by the new accountholder, entered on-line after they left and then filed.

I learned step by step the process and enjoyed my daily customer contact. The feedback and survey comments from my customers were always positive.

Some saying things like "Janet explained everything very well and was nice."

Or, "It was so easy and fast to open our account with Janet."

Or, "Smiled and always so nice."

When I moved to the teller line, it was an easy transition. I had been opening accounts and knew the system. I enjoyed the customer contact and I flourished as I worked with many more customers daily. I enjoyed myself much more than I did in new accounts. Every bank customer was a new opportunity for me to use my WOO. I could small talk and ask questions about their day getting to know them and still keep the line moving. Once I would get repeat customers, I easily developed a rapport and we'd talk about kids, families and what they did on the weekend in the short time they were at my window.

I was the type of teller who still did a large number of transactions daily, yet spent quality time with each customer. My sales goals were easily met and I was a high performer as indicated in our weekly branch reports. I received numerous incentive awards at the branch level.

I remember a co-worker being frustrated with my ability to engage with my customers, talking to them all the time, while I completed their transactions. I'd be laughing, joking, asking questions and determining if we had any other products they needed and rarely made any errors, while I cashed their checks or made deposits.

She would complain that I bothered her and she couldn't concentrate, because I was talking all the time. She felt it was my fault that she couldn't balance at night or make her sales goals and made too many mistakes. She'd make comments like, "Do you ever stop talking, I can't even hear myself think?" "Why do you ask them how there day is going, it's none of your business." When she was out of balance she'd say, "Well if Janet didn't talk to the customers all the time I would be able to concentrate." The supervisor or manager would usually just tell her, "Let's just figure out where you're out of balance so we can all go home."

Luckily, I had a manager that didn't blame me for her outages and mistakes and moved her to the other end of the line when she asked and telling her, "Now you'll have no one else to blame for not being able to balance." She didn't last long and was eventually let go because of her lack of skills; not my talking that distracted her.

This was why I was also a good branch liaison/project coordinator. I was promoted and became part of a team on a huge project to bring check processing in-house. One of my responsibilities was working with the programmers to review the new on-line system the branches would use on a daily basis.

This was a massive project with a brand new system that took months to complete each step. I remember one day I was reviewing a portion of the teller functions and kept getting stuck in this one area. Jim, the system analyst, I was working with was getting frustrated because I kept asking questions and telling him it couldn't work the way he had programmed it. My strategic mind kept trying to find better options and methods to meet the needs of the tellers and stay within the scope of the program.

Every time we'd hit a problem, I'd start asking another set of questions like, "This isn't user friendly for the teller, they need to have a calculation here before they move one."
His response, "Can't have one there."
My response, "Okay, where can we have one?"
His, "That's not in the specs."
Mine, "Well it won't work without one, so can we move it to another section earlier, and then we'll need it later to balance. Again?"
His, "Can't do it."
Mine, "Then this won't work and we'll have to start over."

We went around and around for hours. Back and forth and I would not back down and accept it the way he had programmed it. I finally convinced him my way was the most efficient and logical and he reluctantly used my input and re-wrote that program. It worked perfectly and meet everyone needs. We worked on a number of projects together that year and learned to trust each other and compromise.

I did well and flourished in the banking environment, receiving numerous promotions, finding balance, and the ability to utilize my strengths and skills to the benefit of all. I had many opportunities to work in a number of different areas learning new skills that kept me from getting bored. I had a number of management positions and enjoyed 16 years with the same bank.

###

I usually I know when I have stepped over the edge or am too much for the company I'm in and adjust myself on my own. I'm better at reading others and situations now than when I was younger. It's fun for me now, as I regulate to the situations and know who to have fun with and when to roll with the group.

I was at a business-training workshop once with a couple of co-workers, who both were single and as different as night and day. One was very savvy, well dressed, engaging, a little cynical and very smart. The other one was introverted, shy, mousy, non-decisive and also very smart. We all were there to evaluate a system and come back with our recommendations. We were there for over a week, evaluating during the day and in a hotel at night.

The company wanted our business and it was a long week. It was fun for the first couple of days, then we just all wanted to be done and go home. We had one car and two back seat drivers. We were getting lost all the time and would end up arguing on where to turn. This was before GPS, so we were working with a city map trying to get through construction areas daily. I eventually learned to keep quiet and let them drive and navigate.

One evening we all decided to go out for dinner and hear some music. Yes, we got lost on the way to the restaurant, so nerves were up when we finally arrived. Dinner was a little uncomfortable as one was snarky and accusing and the other one whiney and apologetic. When I tried to change the subject it only made it worse, so I sat back, people watched and tuned them out. That was a roll with it night, that I was relieved when I finally got back to my room. Thankfully, we all had our own rooms.

###

Now, I do want to say that the people who usually want me to tone it down are typically the same people who have relied on me to find out what's going on, ask for directions, make other people feel comfortable, and to be the bold one in the room. I'm just saying that there are times when my type of personality is useful, and people like me are relied on to get the party started or keep it going.

A few years ago, I went out with a group for a girl's night out. There were several of us, and I just happened to be the oldest. We had a great dinner, went to a hockey game and then out dancing. As we would walk into places, most of them had their phones in their hands and were looking down.

Not me. I'm looking around to see if I knew anyone, smiling at people and swaying to the music. I do love to dance. At this one place, the bouncer walked over to our group to ask if we were all having fun and what we were celebrating. He was just being friendly.

I kept the conversation up, joking with him, asking questions like, "What is your full-time job? What do you like about all his jobs? Did you have a family and where do you want to be in five years?"

Just basically chatting. After a few minutes, he hugged me and walked away. The girls were all stunned and wanted to know how I knew him, where we'd previously met and how long I'd known him. Well, I didn't know him until right that moment. We'd just met. I was just being friendly, listening to him, and we connected.

Learning to be interested in others has allowed me to meet so many different and interesting people. You know from past chapters that I wasn't born this way. Using eye contact, reaching out and shaking hands or touching arms, being open, listening and being friendly are traits that I have developed over the years.

My Advice to You:

It doesn't matter how many questions you ask, it's all about listening, connecting and getting to know others. Find a conversation style that you are comfortable with and keep it simple. Just learn to have fun and enjoy yourself. And if you want some books I've used in the past, check the Resource chapter out for some of my favorite books and websites.

These are skills anyone can learn and use, by starting with one, then getting comfortable using it. To me, it all starts with looking someone in the eye while you're smiling. People make decisions on whether they'll like you or want to talk to you in the first few seconds. If you can't look them in the eye, they'll ignore you or walk away. I think this is the hardest part of being in a new situation with people you don't know. Find your comfort zone, even if you have to step out and be bold.

Next, you need a good handshake, something firm, not crushing or wimpy. Shake the whole hand, not just the fingers. Look the person in the eye and smile. Enjoy yourself;

don't act like it's painful, even if it is, as others will realize it and you'll lose your confidence and credibility. If you have to, make a game out of it, and practice with others if it'll help, until it's a comfortable habit.

It's also good to find questions and small talk you're comfortable using. Practice talking out loud or with friends about things that are fun and easy to talk about will help when you are out in public settings. Be the one who can keep a conversation going and is interested in what others have to say. At some point, we all end up in situations that take us out of our comfort zone. It's better to be ready for the awkward and prepared for the difficult. Then everything else is a piece of cake.

Being a good listener is the best way to find out about others. I mean really listen. Actively hear what they're saying and then ask pertinent questions. If you're always preparing your answers or next questions in your mind, you don't really hear what they are saying and you never really connect.

CHAPTER 6
GLASS HALF FULL - POSITIVITY

"Positive anything is better than negative nothing."
~Elbert Hubbard

Dad/Poppy was the most influential person in my life. He was the eternal optimist . . . always a glass half full kind of guy. He believed good thoughts; hard work, a positive outlook and laughter were all it took. To succeed he showed us all that it didn't matter how many times you were knocked down. As long as you got back up and tried again, you would eventually win or move on to better things.

I saw positivity in action, as I watched my parents help others throughout my life. They encouraged, supported, and celebrated life and were always there for my brothers and me. Even when I was my most invisible and my mom at her sickest, I always knew I was loved and cared about with daily infusions of their version of joy and happiness.

Because of my parents' enthusiasm for life, positive attitudes, and caring hearts, we always had someone extra living with us in my teen years. My mom had enormous empathy for any children who were struggling. I think this was due to her difficult childhood. My dad just had a big heart that wanted to help anyone who needed a "hand up", as he would say. Lots of strays . . . kids, family and friends, anyone who needed a little space or a safe place to spend the night. My brothers and I were always bringing someone home with us. Many crashed for the night on the living room floor, some stayed longer and all became lifelong friends.

Ours was the open house, with my parents being called Mom and Pop by all. They were the positive and supportive adults in many of these different peoples' lives. They listened and didn't necessarily try to solve all of the problems unless help was needed. They just showed us all unconditional love.

My dad was always the positive one. I don't ever remember a time he wasn't positive and throughout his lifetime he had many opportunities that tempted his faith. But, he never showed it. For him, choosing to see the good side of each situation was the way he wanted to live his life and show up each day.

I remember one time, when he was in college full-time and working part-time, I woke up in the middle of the night and found him asleep on his books. When I touched his arm, he woke up immediately and pulled me into his arms for a hug. I was thirsty, so he picked me up and we went into the kitchen for a glass of water.

I touched his face because he looked so tired and said to him, "Daddy you need to go to bed you're too tired."

He replied, "I'm okay, I just have to finish this paper." He snuggled my neck and made me giggle, as he put me back to bed. I heard him the shuffling of paper at the table as I went to sleep. He couldn't have slept much those years in college, with a wife and three kids to feed, studying, working and getting his college degree. I never heard him complain about it.

So if any of us started complaining or whining about something not going our way or 'a poor me' attitude, he'd let us go on for a while and sympathize, then we'd get a "Poppism" like:

"Are you done feeling sorry for yourself, there are a lot of people out there a lot worse off than you?"

"What do you have to complain about? You have a roof over your head and food on the table. Many people don't, so be grateful for what you have"

He was good at raising his eyebrow and giving us that look of "Is it really that bad?" and then he'd laugh and share his take on our current dilemma that usually made sense and the reason so many sought him out for council.

Now, if any of us did something wrong or made some mistake, he'd always remind us that we are all a family and a reflection of each other. He would say, "Just don't to shit in your own nest." or ask us, "What did you learn by that dumb mistake?" He'd throw his spin on whatever was happening and still be in our corner as we worked through our individual issues, reminding us all that this was just another life lesson.

**

My mom's life was a little more complicated because she grew up in survival mode from an early age. Her feelings of abandonment began when her mom left. She was 3 years old and living with her dad, who was an alcoholic. Her early life struggles led her to decide, at 13, to move out on her own and get a job at a diner. These events colored her comfort and security for years.

She met my dad on a train the day she left her hometown to start a new life. They were married three months later and celebrated their 57th anniversary before he passed away. He gave her the security, family and love she craved and she gave him her love and a family. However, more importantly, she believed in him and supported his decisions through their lives.

When I was in high school, my mom was ill for several years and had numerous surgeries that she suffered through. Her recoveries were extensive and it took all of her energy, each time, to just take care of herself. She had a string of problems and needed one surgery after another. She was finally healthy shortly after I joined the Air Force and moved away. When we moved back 4 years later it was nice to see her healthy and happy.

Her need to nurture and take care of others was her way of not wanting anyone else to feel forgotten or left out. She knew how that felt. She has championed and been a loyal supporter of children's rights her whole life. She loves going to school events and has been a volunteer for years, just so she can be near the kids. One of her favorite times was when she volunteered to listen to the kids read in elementary school. She got as much joy out of it as the kids did, now whenever she gets a chance, she cherishes her times to read to any of her grandkids and great grandkids. She sends books and stuffed animals yearly to all the young children in her life.

Christmas became her favorite holiday because it gave her a chance to share her love and positivity in the miracle and magic of the season. I believe this is because she never had the celebrations and joy herself when she was young, so she still goes out of her way to make sure everyone is included and no one is alone at the holidays.

My mom organized and ran the community Christmas

program for over 20 years, making sure no families or kids ever went without a holiday dinner or gifts under the tree. Each year, in September after school started, she'd meet with the current principal of the schools to explain about the community program and need for the students to participate and help. Then she would visit all of the businesses and churches to find out how they wanted to participate. She was very protective of her list of families identified by the churches, schools and city, not allowing the list to be public. Once the list was completed she would prepare tags for each child, boy or girl, age and suggestions for gifts. These tags would be placed on the community Christmas tree, in the local bank, allowing people to pull tags and buy gifts for those children.

The students would get involved with the food drive for canned goods for the boxes for each family. Each year, she arranged for a holiday dinner to be prepared in December and invited the seniors and anyone without a family. Finally setting the date and place to wrap all the gifts and divide the food up among all the families to be delivered to City Hall for families to pick up at their convenience the week before Christmas.

She has made it her life's mission to take care of all the kids and always has a soft spot for single families and kids that she feels are being neglected. She is our matriarch; her kids, grandkids and great grandkids all know how much she adores them and how important it is to her to stay connected with each of them. She had to nurture her own positivity as she grew up and hers comes from a different place in her heart.

In the last chapter, I talked about positivity being my number one strength now, however you also know this wasn't always the case. Charm school was the beginning for me on my journey towards positivity. It wasn't a straight route by any means and I still had bouts of depressions and could wallow in the self-pity pit with the best of them.

However, in Charm school I was meeting new people, attended networking events, going to grand openings, or luncheons. I was learning different methods of small talk and how to relax more, enjoy conversations and the company of others. As my confidence grew, so did my positivity.

I didn't blossom overnight into a positive, confident, sassy, independent girl, however I was enjoying all these chances to expand and see what the world had to offer. I wasn't necessarily fearless, but I was enthusiastic and liking the fun and excitement brought on by all the new opportunities I was experiencing.

My wardrobe was one of the first areas that changed immediately since there was a dress code for all students. My clothing choices went from nondescript to more classic and business professional. This was still the early 70's and I was used to wearing mini-shirts, bellbottoms, flowery, flowing blouses and billowy skirts, now I was required to wear women's business attire leaning towards, classic suits and dresses. This was a big change for the whole class and took us several months before we were totally comfortable in our new looks.

One of the biggest changes for all of us was the requirement to wear hats and gloves every day. It was a style used by celebrities, first ladies and in TV series, not necessarily average girls on the street. Styles were still influence by Jackie Kennedy's use of classic simple, elegant designs. Her use of the pillbox hat was still a popular style and I had the cutest pink one just like hers.

In the Downtown area, as we ventured out in groups so often, we became known as the girls from the fashion school.

Well, we did stick out as a group in our hats and gloves; however, what I remember and enjoyed most was that we were encouraged to have fun and be positive, to smile, look people in the eye and connect with others. Since many of us had been hiding and trying to be as invisible as possible, this was often a difficult and scary time for some of us.

Restaurants, stores and businesses were friendly and welcomed us. They became our village that encouraged, supported and protected us. I remember a time when several of us met for breakfast at a local diner near the school. We were all excited for the day, talking and laughing with each other.

The waiter delivered this hand-written note to our table from another diner who basically thanked us for being young, beautiful and excited for our day. He told us he enjoyed watching us having fun, encouraging each other and that he hoped we had a great day, because he was going to, after catching some of our positive energy.

We never knew who wrote that note, but it did make us all feel great that morning, and was something we reminisced about throughout the year.

###

My Advice to You:

Find your balance and what makes you happy. Being positive can be difficult if you don't change your thought processes. Starting each day with what you have to be grateful for can help. Just finding one thing each day that was good and positive will get you started.

Not everyone will always appreciate your sunny disposition, when what he or she really wants to do is complain, curse and be disgruntled. I have learned that some people enjoyed the dark side and refuse to be positive. Then for others, that venting and getting all the negativity out helps them to see the other side and they can find their own silver lining. I've learned you can't make other people positive you can only work on yourself. A couple of my favorite books on positively are "The Power of Positive Thinking" By Norman Vincent Peale and "The Happiness Project" By Gretchen Rubin. See Resources for other book suggestions and links.

So when you have midnight, 2am and/or 4am feedings, sick babies and an important meeting the next morning, putting on a smile, using some humor and being positive will still make the day go easier. Difficult co-workers, employees or bosses who are unreasonable and not fun to work with or for, are tough days for the best of us; however, finding that one positive thing in the day that you can hold on to is so much better for your soul than rehashing a crappy day in details.

Now, I very rarely allow myself to dwell on the negatives. There is something to say about age and wisdom that gives me the ability to look at each day and stay in gratitude for the wonderful gifts I get to enjoy. It's true--life is short, and we never know when our time is going to be up on this earth, so for me, I only want to look at the positive possibilities and how lucky I am to be alive.

Some days you can't change the circumstances only your attitude and choosing a positive one is all on you, so "Choose Wisely".

CHAPTER 7
STRENGTHS VERSUS WEAKNESSES

"Build upon strengths, and weaknesses will gradually take care of themselves."
~Joyce C. Lock

I love this quote -
"Build upon Strengths, and Weaknesses will gradually take care of themselves." This is so true, in so many ways.

When we are young, we spend all our time just trying to figure out how things work. Over and over again, we focus on things we don't know how to do. These are supposed to be our weaknesses, even though no one calls them that until we get older. We're allowed the time to try again and again to perfect a skill. Even that phrase "perfect a skill" indicates that to be good at something, we need to be perfect.

We should not look at the things we're not good at as weaknesses. Why instill that negative thought in our head that we're flawed in some way? Why not consider it one of our least favorite things to do and don't label it at all? There are very few people who are perfect at everything; in fact, I'd go as far as to say no one is perfect. They may be perfect at a lot of things; however, there will be something that they don't enjoy doing or don't like, which usually means they aren't good at it.

Every one of us has something we just don't get and never will. I have lots of things I'd rather not do, like tree trimming. I can do it if I have to, but the tree probably won't look great afterwards, and I have no desire to learn that skill. I don't consider it a weakness; it's just not a desired trait.

I do like gardening, though, and growing flowers, and even weeding. There is something about the fresh air, working with the dirt and the results of blooming plants at different times of the year that I enjoy. It's calming and lets my mind wander. I can tell you, I have settled a number of the world's issues while gardening, in addition to some of my own.

Until recently, I never even knew that strengths were something that had been broken down and could be identified in each person. When I found out that there was an actual test that I could take and it would tell me my top five strengths, I said, "Sign me up."

I heard about this concept at a networking event and learned that over 12 million people have taken this test already. If it was good enough for them, it was good enough for me. The test consisted of a thirty-minute on-line questionnaire relating to the 34 strength themes. Depending on how the questions were answered would determine the top five strengths for each person who took the test. The 34 themes all have a Balcony (good ways strengths are used) and a Basement (how strengths can work in a negative way) about each one and instructions on how to take the test.

The evaluation includes a Personalized Strengths Insights and an Action Planning Guide on each strength, with a Shared Theme Descriptions on your top five, 10 ideas for an action plan, examples of what each theme "sounds like" and steps to help you leverage your talents for achievement.

Below are my Top 5 Strengths of the 34 Themes from the Clifton Strengths Finder (Please see the reference page at the end for the link) -

1. Positivity
2. WOO
3. Maximizer
4. Empathy
5. Strategic

This is how I view my Strengths:

My Number One Strength is Positivity. The Balcony for me is being Positive every day and is my number one focus. I enjoy my sunshine and blue skies world. I love to laugh and spread contagious joy. My open personality and friendly manner makes me approachable and non-threatening. I purposely surround myself with those that are like-minded and look at life with wonderment and excitement. I enjoy complimenting and encouraging others. It makes me feel good when others feel good about themselves. I know from the core of my being that we all have the ability to attain anything we set our minds to if we just believe we can do it.

Now the basement or downside to Positivity is I can appear to be "Pollyannaish" and not in touch with the real world. I choose to emphasis the good things and focus on the positives. I don't think I'm naïve, because I look at the positive side first and don't dwell on gutter stuff. I am sensitive to those that question my sunny side and willing to have deep discussions on unpleasant subjects, however I won't wallow in doom and gloom for long if there are no solutions.

My Number Two Strength is WOO. I covered it a lot in

Chapter Three and talked about my enjoyment in meeting new people and the satisfaction I get from making connections and Winning Others Over. When I'm excited about something my enthusiasm can overtake anything in my path. Either come along and have fun with me or move out of my way. I will never run you over, I'll just try to use my charm to convince you that it'll be fun and you don't want to miss out, however I will never force you and I will gently leave you behind as I go on my merry way.

Now the basement of WOO is that on the surface as I flit from group to group, it appears that I don't care about deep relationship or that I'm fake or shallow. What's happening for me as I meet large groups of people is I gravitate to those that are like-minded. I can tend to move quickly among the different personalities until I find my tribe and those I can connect with.

My Number Three Strength is Empathy. This is my ability to sense the feelings of others because I can imagine myself in their lives or situation. I generally understand their joy, pain, happiness and suffering. I accept this as a strength, because I can easily build trust and innately know what to say to help others.

Empathy is also the one I have to be most careful with, because I can easily get sucked into the drama of others. As an emotional, tenderhearted person, who has been a caregiver her whole life, I want everyone to be happy and healthy. It's taken me years to figure out I can't fix everything and to not get over involved. I still empathize and feel their pain and suffering that usually hurts my heart, however for my own self-care I have learned to walk away and let them learn the lessons attached their circumstance on their own.

My Number Four Strength is Maximizer. This is when I look at something I always want to make it bigger, better, brighter, bolder and to get the maximum benefit out of whatever I'm working on. This includes people, trying to figure out what makes each of us so different. This is one of the reasons I asked so many questions when I meet someone, I like to see how I can help them realize how to get the most out of their talents. This is why I focus on what I'm good at and not my shortcomings. I'd rather concentrate on my good qualities and enhance them, than invest anytime on my flaws.

Now the downside to being a Maximizer is that I tend to want perfectionism. I have been known to keep working on a project, by tweaking and make small changes, until others involved tell me "That's enough." "This is what we wanted, nothing more, and it is perfect as it is, so leave it alone." You're "Too Picky!" and "It's never good enough for you, you always have to find one more thing." I can also sabotage my own efforts by failing to launch an idea and going with what I have, because I think it's not good enough.

My Number Five Strength is Strategic. I'm able to look at the big picture to make sure I find the best path or method to use. I look at all avenues and ways to get something done and determine the best route. This distinct way of thinking allows me to see patterns where others see complexity. I like the problem solving and playing out alternative scenarios, kind of like my own a maze head game. It's why I'm so inquisitive and a "What If" type of person. I have to keep asking questions, so I can visualize the different outcomes.

Now the hard part for me is when I'm trying to share my thoughts and unable to get others to follow my convoluted train of thought. It'll make perfect sense to me, but I can have a hard time getting others to buy into my solution. I have been accused of jumping to conclusions, when actually I'm figuring out how to solve a puzzle. Because I'm persistent and by using my other strengths, I can eventually can get my point across.

My Advice to You:

Take the Clifton Strengths Finder evaluation now.

Don't miss the opportunity to find out what your strengths are and understand how to utilize and leverage each of them to your advantage. See Resources for classes you can attend and receive hands on training on the best uses.

Focus on what you love and what speaks to your heart, and follow that path using your natural talents and skills to create a fulfilled life.

Find those things in your life that give you pleasure, that make you feel good. Try all kinds of different projects and tasks to help you decide what you're good at and can't wait to do again. Plus, it helps you to stay away from those areas that are more tedious and drain you more than energize you, and something you can have fun doing. Delegate those not-so-fun chores, if they are necessary to your daily livelihood or health, and free yourself to be creative and fulfilled.

This is really useful with children and family members whose individual strengths you've identified, so everyone can focus on those rather than trying to improve areas they're just not interested in. The sooner kids start to find activities they enjoy and begin developing their skills, the better their self-confidence becomes, and the more likely they are to try new ones. It's also better to identify what doesn't thrill them and let them move on, versus keeping them in something they don't have fun with even though they may excel at it.

There are always going to be family projects and events that not all of us like to do, whether it's cleaning the house, going to visit relatives, the dentist, etc., that are still necessary and unavoidable. We all have these days and are wise when we plan a fun event to happen after the difficult ones.

The same goes for volunteering our loved ones or ourselves--make sure you find things you or they enjoy doing. It'll make the experience that much more rewarding and something we would do again. As we introduce our kids to the world of giving, either time or money, those areas we can relate to or that speak to our hearts are the ones we'll stay connected with throughout our lives versus something we dread doing.

Our businesses and family lives will improve and be healthier when we focus more on what we are good at than on what we avoid. When we spend our time and energy on things that really matter to us, our lives, attitudes and interactions with others will become uplifting and encouraging.

By focusing on what we love and are good at, we learn to live in a place of bold confidence where we don't second guess ourselves and care less about what others think of us. When we work from our strengths versus our weaknesses, we tend to do our best work and make our biggest contributions.

Janet Ravenscraft

CHAPTER 8
SEE ME NOW

"When you become a person of a certain age, whatever that age is for you, life becomes all about you, and when that happened for me, I refused to rein myself in."
~Janet Ravenscraft

Never Too Late

"As long as you're breathing, it's never too late to do some good."
~Maya Angelou

Whenever I hear the terms "you're too much, too late, too young, too old, too smart, too nice" or whatever, I argue, "by whose standards?" I think it's an arbitrary statement that is just the opinion of the person stating it. What one person may think is too much, the next will think is not enough.

In reference to being too late, you may be able to be too late for an appointment, or a bus, or dinner; however, I don't think any of us can ever be too late to start over, to say you're sorry, or to be kind. *It's never too late to listen to your heart.*

When you become a person of a certain age, whatever that

age is for you, time becomes very important to you. The moment that you actually stop and look around, you really stop and see where you are, you realize you're 30, 40, 50, 60, 70 years old and can't figure out how that happened. *It's never too late to stop and look at your current situation.*

I have actually had these defining moments several times in my life, so far. It's when I have stopped for short periods of time, reflected and started on some other path or another direction. Depending on the current situations, I have changed jobs, moved across the country, switched careers, started a family, created a new business or reinvented myself. *It's never too late to take an adventure.*

Some of my defining moments and adventures were spontaneous, others intentional, some even necessary, and often in an effort to protect and provide for my family. What I never really did was stop and figure out what I wanted. Remember, I wasn't brought up to have passion and purpose, I just moved from one job or situation to the next, always taking everyone else's needs into consideration. *It's never too late to make changes in careers.*

I've already established that I wasn't the most secure, outgoing, grab the world by the tail, ready to run out and make a name for myself kind of girl. I had my WOO by the time I was married and started my first real career and family, yet I was still ruled by my beliefs and conditionings. As a woman, wife and mother, I felt it my responsibility to take care of everyone else's needs before my own. *It's never too late to create balance in your life.*

At one point, when my kids were young, I was working full-time, going to college part-time (and there was no such thing as on-line courses, I had to attend college classes at night), running a house, paying bills, grocery shopping, attending kids' school and sports events, everything all of us parents do, and didn't even realize that I had no time for myself. Lucky for me, I had a great husband, who often carried more than his share of household and childcare responsibilities. I still didn't have any time for myself. *It's never too late to find time for yourself.*

We never really had very many personal goals or even a budget, we just tried to pay our bills with what we made and hoped we didn't have any major things break down at the same time. You see, I knew how to set business goals, I went through that process every year; however, I only had a very few personal goals. *It's never too late to start a budget.*

In fact, I remember turning 30 and having one of those defining moments, feeling, "Is this all there is?" This was because my goals from the last 10 years were to get married, own a home and have my kids by the time I was 30. I had done it and didn't even realize that I didn't have any other personal goals. I was depressed when I realized I had accomplished those goals. I asked myself, "Now what?" Then I realized *it's never too late to set new goals.*

But I didn't set any new goal. I was just too busy. I didn't have time to dwell on that for very long, so I just forced myself to get over it and went back to letting my life just happens again. My marriage was secure, I had a great husband, kids were growing up, had family and friends, built a house, had a good job (that was at least interesting, even if I didn't love it), we had busy lives and just lived. *It's never too late to slow down.*

The next BIG change/defining moment came after I had been in a car accident. So many things could have happened that day that didn't, and my life and the lives of my two passengers were spared. I was heading to our monthly managers meeting and had picked up two other managers on the way. I was driving on an eight-lane road, four lanes coming and going, when I crested a hill and saw the traffic was stopped before me.

I began applying my brakes and was going to stop without any problems, until I looked in my rear view mirror. All I could see the grill of a one-ton truck and nothing more. I was in one of the middle lanes and in a split second I looked to my left.

Not seeing any cars, I cocked my steering wheel slightly to the left just before the impact. The truck hit the rear end of my Maxima and we did a 180-degree slide across two lanes, and stopped in the median. We hadn't hit anyone else and no one else hit us. Plus, we weren't crushed between a one-ton truck and a car that was in front of me.

To this day, I believe it was divine intervention that we landed in the median, in the middle of an eight-lane road and with no fatalities. What else would you call it? It sent me into an emotional tailspin as I recovered from the trauma and depression. I was out on medical leave for several months as I received physical and cognitive therapy. Luckily both of my passenger recovered their injuries, however the guilt I had because I was driving made it difficult to carpool or drive anyone else in my car for years. When I could focus again, I wanted a change. *It's never too late to start over and change directions.*

This led to us buying a Hardware Store in Idaho, quitting our jobs, selling our houses, packing everything up and moving all in a three-month period of time. Again, with divine intervention, as we knew no one and went on a pure leap of faith that everything would work out for the best, we moved. *It's never too late to take a leap of faith.*

I tell people we looked like the Beverly Hillbilly Clampetts when we moved lock, stock and lots of barrels that summer. My dad, son and cats were in an old 30-foot camper, towing his Subaru, with one brother and his dog in an old panel van and my youngest brother in his jeep. We sent them out two days before the rest of us, as we knew they would be slower. We followed them. My husband was driving the U-Haul, towing his truck. My Mom had another cat in her car. And myself and our daughter were in my car. Everyone met at the Idaho border and drove to the middle of Idaho in a six-vehicle train. We were definitely a sight pulling into our new hometown on that hot summer day. *It's never too late to take a family road trip.*

We owned that hardware store for 11 years, which gave us the opportunity to build a business, work together as a family, and spend more time with our kids as they grew up. It was an awesome time to live in a very small community, earn the trust and respect of the locals, and then, when we sold the store, it allowed my parents to retire and pay their house off. *It's never too late to help your parents achieve their goal.*

Once we sold the hardware store, our kids were both in college, so we moved near them and started over again in Boise, Idaho. John stayed in retail and sales for the next 10 years, while I started working for a title company. In fact, I planned on retiring for that company until my department was downsized and I was laid off. *It's never too late to come to another crossroad and figure out which way you want or need to go next.*

The last two years have been transformational. When I was laid off, I was waiting for a second eye surgery. Unfortunately, that surgery didn't correct my vision problem and nothing else was available, so I was definitely at another crossroad. I tried a couple of direct selling opportunities, that just weren't fun for me and decided I needed to stop and determine what I really wanted to do next. I had been networking for several months and people were talking about passion and purpose and I had no idea that I should be able to pursue my passions or what it was. *It's never too late to find your passion and purpose.*

This year I hired a business coach who helped me looked at my life. She continually asked me questions until I could define those things that mattered to me most and what made me want to get up every morning and do. I decided this would be my year to say yes to everything that came into my life. I didn't want to miss anything and wanted to try everything. *It's never too late to just say yes.*

One of the questions asked early on was, "Have you ever wanted to write a book?" I immediately answered, "No, I don't even like to journal!" Then a month later, when I was working through another set of questions and worksheets looking at my life, I decided I wanted to write a book. No one was more surprised than me, but I had a title and chapters and began writing. My writing flowed fairly easily and I thought I was done, until I friend of mine pointed out that it felt like I stopped often and it didn't feel like I was telling the whole story and parts were missing. I could publish it the way it was, however if I really wanted to connect with my readers that maybe I wanted to look at it again. *It's never too late to finish your story.*

So the girl who had created a life of blue skies and sunshine stopped and looked at some of the dark sides of her past life and finished her story. I did go back and look at why I felt a need to be invisible, why I was shy, why I didn't feel like I was good enough. Then I looked at my loneliness and my depression years; all those parts that I had stuffed in corners and cubbies and pulled them out and dealt with them. Some were painful, some easy to understand and others just needed to be looked at let go. *It's never too late to review and process the past so you can move forward and be ready for the future without old baggage.*

My Advice to You:

It is never too late to look at your life and head in another direction. Don't be afraid of the unknown or your past. We all have our own stuff; every single one of us and it's like no one else's. Yes, there will be pieces and parts similar, but your stuff happened to only you.

Take that stuff out periodically and look at it. Decide if any of it still has a hold on your present. Find your peace and what makes you get out of bed every day excited to start your day.

Just do whatever it takes to find new dreams and don't give up!

Here are some "Never Too Late" well known people:

Ray Kroc - McDonald Founder
Until 52 sold paper cups and milkshake mixers
Mary Kay Ash – Mary Kay Founder
Until 45 sold books and home goods door to door
Andrea Bocelli – Singer
Until 33 piano players in bars
Ang Lee, Film Producer
Until 31 jobless house husband
J.K. Rowling- Author Harry Potter Series
Until 31 single mom on welfare
Harrison Ford– Actor and Producer
Until 30 a carpenter
Suze Ortman – Financial Advisor and Speaker
Until 30 a waitress

Discover Me Mode

"There are two great days in a person's life, the day we are born and the day we discover why."
~William Barclay

I have been discovering things about myself my whole life

and, as I have aged, there has always seemed to be something missing. I didn't know what it was, so I just kept searching for it. Those times when life slowed down for a few moments or another defining moment smacked me in the face, I would get a glimpse of something shiny, different and somewhat mystical, and then it would be gone.

Just when I thought that I'd be able to retire in a few years, my life hit another speed bump. For some reason, the vision in my left eye started getting distorted. I ignored it as long as I could, thinking it was my cataract. Then as it became increasingly harder to read contracts and work on the computer, I went to the have it checked out.

Two eye surgeries later, thousands of dollars and several months of recovery time did not correct my vision problem. I talked about being laid off in section 'Never Too Late'. I was in the middle of those two surgeries, not ready to retire, and now had to find another job.

I did the rounds of seeing all the specialists again, and none of them knew why my vision was distorted, just that their surgeries were successful. Great, I now I had a repaired retina, a replaced cataract and no further options. At this point, I was done with doctors and decided to get on with my life.

The hardest part was that I was no longer able to perform the job I had been doing for the last ten years. All of that close-up work--reading contracts and documents on the computer all day--was something I wouldn't be able to do any longer. Now what to do? What do I want to do? Not want to do?

I started going to job fairs, workshops, seminars, networking events, just to see what was out there, what I was qualified to do. I started meeting all these amazing women and men living their dreams, talking about passion and purpose, with goals and action plans, just having fun. I didn't know what it was, but I knew I wanted some of it.

I wanted something that I could get excited about, something that made me want to get out of bed each morning, raring to go with a plan, make money doing something I was actually good at and that spoke to my heart. I still didn't have any idea what it was, but I was ready to try anything.

I was drawn to the entrepreneurial, self-employed, work-for-yourself aspect. I even tried direct sales for a short period of time. I totally believed in my service, and I'll have it for life. I even believed in the business model, that the service would sell itself. My problem was that I felt like a stalker with the whole "follow-up until they buy, because when they say no, they really don't mean no, they just mean not right now."

Hey, when I say "no" or "I'm not interested," I mean it, and you can check back with me, but I don't want someone to keep bugging me. I couldn't work the sales process and I was miserable, so I stopped. I made the decision it wasn't for me. I thoroughly appreciate those in direct sales and multi-level marketing, as it's not for the soft-hearted. I support my fellow entrepreneurs' products and services that I want in my life. I also have said "no or I'm not interested" more times than I have said "yes," and have no desire to work in that world again.

This is when I started on my Discover Me journey. I purposely started to interview and ask everyone I met, "What he or she liked about what they were doing?" "Why they did it?" "Where they saw themselves in one year to five years?" "Did they have a legacy?" And, finally, "When they pictured themselves successful doing something they loved, what did it look and feel like to them?"

After a couple of months of this, I decided I couldn't do it on my own, and hired a business coach. Best decision I ever made!! She helped me focus, look at my life, and kept asking me questions until I found my answers that came from my heart and soul. All that stuff that was buried, deep down-- things I liked to do, what I was drawn to and good at, what my family and friends thought I was good at and depended on me to do.

My Advice to You:

Step out of your comfort zone and find what your passions and purposes are hiding within you.

I am truly grateful that I was able to stop, examine my life, invest in myself and hire a business coach to walk with me through this process. My Discover Me journey was Exhilarating, Enlightening and has Energized me to step out and be Epic. It's never too late to stop and take your own Discover Me journey. My goals now are to Have Fun, Share my Passion and Travel the World.

Here's a sample of questions from my 15-minute strategy session.

1. Imagine – What your life looks like when you're doing something you enjoy?
2. Now - What's your life like now?
3. Proud - What are you proud of now?
4. Gap - Can you see the gap from where you are now to where you want to go?
5. Stopping You – What's stopping you from getting there?
6. Needs to Happen – What needs to happen next?
7. Possibilities – What are some different possibilities that you can work on?
8. Close Gap – What's it going to take to close the gap between where you are and where you want to go?

9. Recap – Let's recap what we've talked about and come up with three things you can do today.

It was eye opening and painful at times, getting to the root of my feelings, hopes and desires that I had stuffed and kept closed off and hidden from the world and myself. Those periods of my life that were responsible for my beliefs and how I look at life now were insightful and significant to my growth and where I'm heading now.

I did decide a year ago I wouldn't say no to anything that came my way. If I really wanted to explore and know myself better I would also need to be fearless. My passion now is to encourage, empower and enlighten others to discover their passions and realize it's is never too late.

This year I have accomplished:

- Wrote a Book – this is my first book that became a soul search and labor of love. Everyone has a story to tell are you ready to write yours. Take Renee Settle's 12 Minute Day Workshop to get you started.

- Volunteering -helped a number of organizations with events, projects conferences and workshops including; Idaho Laugh Fest, Habitat of Humanity and Women Ignite. Giving back is the best way to make a difference. Find an organization or program your whole family can volunteer together and give back to your community. Best way to show children how it's done.

- Conferences and Workshops - in Arizona, California, Nevada and Idaho for Idaho Women Business Owners, Women Ignite, Boles University, Legal Shield, Meet and Mingle, Women of Wisdom and Inspiration, Frank White International, Local

Impact Zone, 10 Men Standing. There are conference and workshops on any subject, project, business opportunities, hobbies or that could educate and inform you.

- On-line Webinars and Teleseminars - by Patricia Noel Drain, Tom Antion, Darren Hardy, Deepak Chopra, Oprah, Brendon Burchard, Russell Brunson, Arianna Huffington and Renee Settle. There are thousands of On-line webinars and Teleseminars that are available daily that could provide a wealth of information and you may learn something new.

- Personal Development Books - I've read over 30 personal development books this year. Goal was to read two a month and I belonged to the Branded Book Club. Every successful person I know declare that reading personal development material daily is what pushed them to the next level. Never stop learning.

- Mastermind and Accountability groups - monthly group interaction to improve our businesses and have accountability partners. Join a mastermind group that will encourage, support and help you work and improve your business, then find an accountability partner or group that will hold you responsible for your goals and projects.

- Certified Coach - Your Gift is Your Niche program that helped me find out what I wanted to do next. If anyone is ready to find out what their gift or passions are, go to my website and sign up for my 6 module, one-on-one program.

- Video Challenges – participated in two video

challenges this year learning how to take videos, develop content, improve on-line presence and upload videos to Facebook and YouTube. Learn to make your own videos, be comfortable in front of a camera, upload to YouTube, Facebook, etc.

- Speaker – Take Action Speech at the Arizona Conference, Discover Me Speech at Idaho Women Business Owners Luncheon, Backup Speaker- gave another speakers presentation when she was unable to do it herself. If you want to be a speaker, take some classes, join a Toastmasters group, and attend workshops. If you need a motivational speaker for your next conference, workshop or meeting, please contact me through my website. This is my favorite part of my business.

- On-line Email List and newsletter – I created an on-line list and published a newsletter. If you want to be an entrepreneur or own your own business, then creating your own email list is a must. It's the only list that is completely you. Do your research and find one that will meet your needs.

- Self Defense and Gun lessons - took a Self-defense class, bought a gun and learned how to shoot it. Expand your knowledge and learn a new skill every few months. These were life skills I had never had an opportunity to take, so decided I would this year. I hope you will do something that interest you. Stretch and step out of your comfort zone every now and then.

- Branded 100% Program – Currently working through the business and marketing program. Take classes, course and programs that you can learn new skills or update your existing ones.

- Ran a 5K – ran my first ever 5k in Riggins, Idaho in 2014 and my 2nd in Boise in 2015. If you've never run a 5K it's a rush when you cross the finish line after all the training and effort you put into getting yourself there. It was an awesome feeling.

- Dance Class – bought my first pair of cowgirl boots and took my first Country Swing dance class. Take any kind of dance class, just to get out and do something different and its great exercise. If you're trying to find something to do with your spouse or partner, she would love it if you surprised her with lessons you signed up to do together.

Refuse to Rein Myself In

"When you become a person of a certain age, whatever that age is for you, life becomes all about you, and when that happened for me, I refused to rein myself in."
~ Janet Ravenscraft

A number of years ago, I figured out that if I didn't start taking care of my own needs first, I would never be able to truly take care of anyone else in my life. I had to think of myself first and find what made me happy, secure, energized, involved, and worthy before I could support those around me, including my family, friends and co-workers.

My years in the corporate world taught me many things. I spent 16 years in the banking industry, which is still a pretty staid, buttoned-down environment, with lots of rules and regulations.

Since it's been established that I have a louder than normal voice and laugh, plus my big personality--let's just say, it wasn't always appreciated by the conservative, controlled corporate world.

Of course, as I explained earlier, these were all the same people who relied on me to use all of my skills, when they wanted teams, groups, branches, offices and departments to get fired up, excited, motivated or involved in the latest project, product or whim of the company.

Managers and mentors at the time explained that if I wanted to be promoted and move up in their world, I would need to be more professional and tone myself down. I was a quick learner who listened, took opportunities when presented and received numerous promotions and new assignments. I worked long hours in often stressful situations and was relied on for my skills and knowledge.

Once I moved into management, it was a constant battle for me to jump back and forth between these realms basically on demand and depending on which manager wanted what. The better managers encouraged and supported my personality and management style, while the weaker ones penalized and tried to change me.

When I became bored or wanted a change, I went out and found or manifested another job, career or business. I always knew when it was time to move on and start new at something else. When my vision started deteriorating, I was working towards retirement. I had been with the same company for 10 years, just had my one-month sabbatical and had four years until I wanted to retire.

When I wasn't able to perform that job any longer, yet still needed to work, I was filled with anxiety and had lots of sleepless nights. I prayed a lot and tried to stay positive as I knew I was exactly where I was supposed to be, and I just tried to be ready for that next door or window to open.

As I was working through the process of what I didn't

want to do again or next, and trying to figure out what kinds of jobs I was actually qualified for, it became increasingly frustrating. Then I figured out it would take two jobs to replace my one income.

That's when I realized that I really didn't want just another job until I retired. What I really wanted was to find something I was passionate about that I could do for the rest of my life. I needed to change my mentality from the whole "work until you retire or die" and instead find something that was fun to do. Something that would allow me to share my passions and travel the world. Whatever it was, needed to create a constant stream of income, allowing me to be independent, self-sufficient and successful.

In addition, this something would have to let me be me. It would have to let my personality shine, glow, reflect and not be reined in. I refuse to apologize or tone myself down any longer. I am who I am, and I will surround myself with those who love and appreciate my gifts and talents. No more standing back and worrying about being too old, too loud, too much. This is not the way I want to live my life any longer.

I'm amazed at how my life has changed in the last year and how many quantum leaps of faith I have taken so far. When you become a person of a certain age, whatever the age, you begin to realize how short life is. I'm at the point where I don't want to miss anything.

My mantra this year has been to say yes to everything. If someone asks me to do something I have done it. I won't kid you it has been scary some days, but what's the worst that can happen. I actually fail? So what, unless its life threatening it's all a learning lesson and as long as I do my best and make it fun I can't lose. Even if I totally bomb at something it's still not the end of the world and I can still stand tall and say I still tried.

My Advice to You:

Be you. Don't be stopped by what others think. You can do whatever, be whoever and go wherever you want. In reality, we are only on this earth for a very short period of time, so do not waste that time worrying about what someone else will think.

I refuse to let other opinions of me keep me from pursuing new ideas, stretching my boundaries, experiencing life, or learning the multitude of technology that is changing every day. I urge you to do the same thing. You have the ability to accomplish anything you set your mind to do. Don't limit yourself.

As I finished my book, I was feeling vulnerable about putting my life out there in print and thinking about who would want to read my book. After all, it's just a story about me. I even asked myself, "What are you afraid of?" But, I have come too far and refuse to stop now, regardless of what happens, this is my story and it deserves to be told. It doesn't deserve to be stuffed in a drawer.

I know there are people who have had similar experiences to mine. But our stories will never be the same. Your story is just as important and life changing as mine. Our stories will resonate with those who have thought all their life that no one knows how they feel or that they're the only one who has had this happen. It's not true. We all need to stop and tell our story so we can move forward and live the life that was intended for each of us.

Don't let anyone stop you from living your dream. Keep your dreams alive and every day take one step toward them.

If you accomplished all of your dreams, then dream bigger dreams. Don't stop coming up with fantastic adventures, full of energy and excitement. Keep your mind open and thoughts flowing creating a life full of wonder and magic and abundance and joy and love!

Live by the following credo:

You are amazing.

You are wonderful.

You are important.

You are beautiful.

I lived by the following words this last year. I have been:

- Bold.
- Fearless.
- Unstoppable.
- Passionate.
- Courageous.
- Committed.
- Purposeful.
- Open.
- Unlimited.
- Consistent.
- Honest
- Epic.

Live your life to the fullest and be thankful each day for those you love and those that love you. That's priceless!!

CHAPTER 9
INFORMATION FOR YOU

Chapter 1:

Moving with Kids Psych Central
From www.psychcentral.com/lib/moving-with-kids/

Moving and Young Children Psych Central
From www. psychcentral.com/lib/moving-and-young-children/

Helping Children Adjust to a Move
Form https://www.healthychildren.org/English/family-life/family-dynamics/Pages/Helping-Children-Adjust-to-a-Move.aspx

Smooth Move: Make Moving Easier on You and Your Kids
From http://www.parents.com/parenting/money/buy-a-house/make-moving-easier-on-you-and-your-kids/

Chapter 2:

Suicide Prevention Hotline
From www.suicidepreventionlifeline.org

24h Teen Suicide Hotlines
From www.teenlineonline.org

The Society for the Prevention of Teen Suicide
From www.sptsusa.org/

Teen Suicide is Preventable
From http://www.apa.org/research/action/suicide.aspx

Teens - Suicide Prevention Resource Center
http://www.sprc.org/sites/sprc.org/files/Teens.pdf

Suicide Prevention Resource Center
http://www.sprc.org/

Chapter 3:

http://hearstcastle.org/history-behind-hearst-castle/art/

Final Touch Finishing School
From www.finaltouchschool.com/

Institut Villa Pierrefeu
From www.ivpworld.com/

Chapter 4:

Stand Up America and Stand Beautiful with Derrick Boles.
From www.standupglobal.org

Navy
From www.navy.com/

U.S. Army
From www.armyenlist.com/

Air National Guard
From www.goang.com/Recruiting

Armed Forces Recruiting
From www.airforce.com/jobs

Chapter 5:

How Planes Fly
'When the plane flies horizontally, lift from the wings exactly balances the plane's weight. But the other two forces do not balance: the thrust from the engines pushing forward always exceeds the drag (air resistance) pulling the plane back. That's why the plane moves through the air .May 3, 2015'
How planes work | the science of flight - Explain that Stuff
From www.explainthatstuff.com/howplaneswork.html

Chapter 6:

None

Chapter 7:

The Clifton Strengths Finder
From www.gallupstrengthscenter.com

Sheli G. StrengthsFinder Workshop
From www.shelig.com

Chapter 8:

12-Minute A Day, Writing for the Non-writer
From www.12minutestory.com

Janet Ravenscraft

CHAPTER 10
BOOK RECOMMENDATIONS

I Love Myself – By Patricia Noel Drain

You Are a Badass - By Jen Sincero

The 7 Habits of Highly Effective People – By Stephen R. Covey

The Ignited Entrepreneur - Sheli G. & Terilee Harrison

Courage to Lead – By Derrick Boles

God Tweets- By Paulette Esposito

Who Moved My Cheese? – By Spencer Johnson, M.D.

Power of Positive Thinking – Norman VincentPeale

"I Get To" - By Joan Endicott

Happiness Project – Gretchen Rubin

Thrive – By Arianna Huffington

The Entrepreneur Rollercoaster – By Darren Hardy

The Quantum Leap Strategy – by Price Pritchett, Ph.D.

DEDICATION

In Memory and Appreciation of Coach Bud Aubuchon

Coach Aubuchon was my first mentor before I even knew what a mentor was all about. He was a teacher and a coach, when I was in high school, who loved what he chose as his profession and was good at it.

Our associate was an unlikely alliance, as I was no athlete or in any of his classes. Plus, he was the head football coach, while I was an awkward, shy, young girl who often felt invisible.

We met when he was the advisor for the school's Booster Club and I was a member. He listened, allowed me to be creative, showed interest and trusted my instincts. He taught me to be self-sufficient and anticipate things before they happened.

He always acknowledged my efforts and encouraged me to try different ways. I am forever grateful for his attention and influence at a time in my life that was confusing and often lonely.

After high school, I began the journey to become a confident, sassy, fearless woman who truly believes it's never too late. I now know that there are a lot of teacher and coaches in the world that give above and beyond and never know how instrumental they were in making a difference!

Thank you to Coach Aubuchon and all the other educators and coaches who give of yourselves every day.

Janet Ravenscraft

ABOUT THE AUTHOR

Janet Ravenscraft is an author, speaker and business owner. She is the founder of the "It's Never Too Late" workshop and creator of the Discovery Me program.

In her Corporate Career, she held numerous management positions, before she started over as an entrepreneur, on a quest to find her passions and purpose.

Her first book SEE ME NOW recounts her invisible journey to her current invincible self.

Janet lives in Idaho with her husband John and near her two grown children. She loves to travel using her passport and spending time with her family.
You can find out more about her by going to her website, www.janetravenscraft.com.

Janet Ravenscraft

Made in the USA
Charleston, SC
04 May 2016